Cuba: A Day in the Life

Stan Dotson

Parson's Porch Books

Cuba: A Day in the Life

ISBN: **Softcover 9780692715987**

Copyright © 2016 by Stan Dotson

All rights reserved. No part of this book may be reproduced or transmitted in any form or by any means, electronic or mechanical, including photocopying, recording, or by any information storage and retrieval system, without permission in writing from the publisher.

Excerpts from "One Today: A Poem for Barack Obama's Presidential Inauguration January 21, 2013" by Richard Blanco, © 2013. Reprinted by permission of the University of Pittsburgh Press.

All other brief citations fall under fair use guidelines.

All photos by Stan Dotson unless otherwise noted

To order additional copies of this book, contact:

Parson's Porch Books
1-423-475-7308
www.parsonsporch.com

Parson's Porch Books is an imprint of Parson's Porch & Company (PP&C) in Cleveland, Tennessee. PP&C is an innovative company which raises money by publishing books of noted authors, representing all genres. All donations from contributors and profits from publishing are shared with the poor.

Cuba: A Day in the Life

Acknowledgements

We know that it's going to change our lives.
—Mariela Castro Espín, December 17, 2014, *Mesa Redonda* interview

As a mountaineer who has lived most of my life in western North Carolina, I can say that spending close to a full year in the exotic landscape of Cuba would surely have been enough, in and of itself, to turn my world upside down. Being there, though, during the historic year when the Cold War between our two countries ended, that was life-changing beyond measure. I am eternally grateful for all who made this conversion experience possible, and appreciate having a platform to share some of the stories.

For any errors or misunderstandings found in this book, and there are bound to be a fair number, the author is solely to blame. It comes with the cross-cultural territory. For any genuine insights or discoveries found here, many people share in the credit. On the U.S. side, many thanks to our families who so generously and graciously supported our journey with their full blessing, and who took on our home responsibilities for us while we were away. Also thanks to our church communities: Ecclesia Baptist in Fairview, the Circle of Mercy in Asheville, Wake Forest Baptist in Winston-Salem, and the larger family of the Alliance of Baptists and the Baptist Peace Fellowship, who have been so faithful in fostering and growing a new model of partnerships with Cuban churches.

On the Cuban side, I also have many to thank. Deep appreciation goes to our Cuban families, especially those living in the two communities where our roots sank deepest: Matanzas and La Vallita. Thanks to Paco and Lila for being our Cuban parents, Orestes and Wanda for being our Cuban siblings and neighbors, and thanks to Sila and Cheo for making their home ours and for giving us the great blessing of so many Cuban nieces and nephews. Thanks to our church communities, especially the Rivers of Living Water Baptist Church in La Vallita and the First Baptist Church of Matanzas, along with the larger family of the Fraternity of Baptist Churches of Cuba, who have accompanied U.S. churches for more than twenty-five years and who have guided us in how to forge sustainable and mutual partnerships. Thanks also goes to our community of family and friends at the Ecumenical Theological Seminary in Matanzas, the students, faculty, administration, and staff who so graciously allowed us the opportunity to teach and learn and live alongside them.

I am tempted to list every person who so deeply touched our hearts with their hospitality, generous spirits, and gracious patience in teaching us how we could discover the treasures of Cuban life and culture without being too intrusive, without being too "North American." Such a list, though, and the stories that accompany each name, would be long enough to fill another book. There is my next project!

Most of all, I give my deepest and most heartfelt thanks to my spouse, soul-mate, and partner in this Cuban adventure. Thanks, Kim Christman, for starting the journey twenty-three years ago when you first ventured to Cuba. Thanks for sharing the ride, and for making the memories. Thanks for listening so intently as I read to you the first draft of each of these chapters, and for giving good feedback and suggestions for improvements. *Te amo, eternamente te amo.*

*dedicated to Edgar Douglas Christman and Jesse Dal Dotson
two coffee lovers who would have loved Cuba*

Preface

*Today, the United States of America
is changing its relationship with the people of Cuba.*
–U.S. President Barack Obama, December 17, 2014

Since my election as President of the State Council I have reiterated on many occasions our willingness to hold a respectful dialogue with the United States on the basis of sovereign equality, in order to deal reciprocally with a wide variety of topics without detriment to the national independence and self-determination of our people.
–Cuban President Raúl Castro, December 17, 2014

Dime con quien andas, y te diré quien eres.
(Tell me who you associate with, and I will tell you who you are.)
–Cuban expression

I began writing this book on a rainy night in August 2015, eight months to the day from the historic speeches of these two Presidents, signaling a thaw in diplomatic relations after fifty-six years of Cold War enmity. It was almost three months after my return home from an eleven-month stay in Cuba with my spouse, Kim. December 17, a date stuck right in the middle of our stay, could well prove to be one of Cuba's most celebrated dates, establishing its place in the history of a Caribbean country whose calendar is already filled with many red-letter days. We could not have chosen a more interesting or significant chunk of time to be there, given the tremendous changes that the completely unexpected December announcement began to unleash.

With all the stories of the year still percolating in my mind, like strong, fresh roasted Cuban coffee grounds brewing in a stovetop *cafetera*, I finally resolved on that August day to go home and start pouring them out onto the page (the computer screen, to be more precise). I turned into the driveway in the late afternoon and got within shouting distance of our home on "The Old Place," our name for the plot of Appalachian mountain land that has been in my family for generations. As it turned out, shouting distance was as close as I could get. Three large trees lying over the road hindered further progress.

An old locust had been the first to fall, and its downfall caught two sweet birches on the way to the ground, uprooting both of them. Looking at the obstacle, I listened to my good old U.S. of A. cultural instinct: launch into problem-solving mode. I walked to the house, changed clothes, and carried down the chainsaw for a couple of hours of clearing brush, cutting the obstructing trunks into manageable lengths, and moving them out of the way.

Near the end of the work, thoughts of how my friends in Cuba would have done it differently entered my mind. For one thing, the work would have taken much longer, as the tools at hand would have been machetes and axes. For another thing, it would have been a community enterprise; no one there does this kind of thing solo. To be fair, I could have opted for collaboration. I have good neighbors, retired folks who would have jumped at the chance to crank up their power tools and cut away. They have done it before, when I have been in a pinch and really needed assistance. For whatever reason, though, I did not think about asking them that afternoon. I was well into the job when I stopped to realize how work in our culture is so often a lonely business.

After clearing the drive, I walked back into the woods to take a look at the root system that had been wrenched out of the ground. It was an impressive sight to see, how strong and widespread the roots had to be to keep such towering structures upright. Being metaphor-minded, I immediately thought of the well-established root systems that have kept our economic embargo and other towering structures of hostility in place. These roots are deeper than the 1959 Triumph of the Revolution and its attendant nationalization of U.S. operated industries. They can be traced back through five hundred years of history between our two lands, starting with European conquest and colonization, on to agricultural exploitation and slave rebellion, wars of independence and U.S. intervention, puppet governments and Mafia playgrounds. Many, many years of prayer and partnership work between church leaders and other people of good will proved to be a soaking rain on the ground of all these structural injustices, until finally, on December 17, an uprooting began to be felt.

There was something personal as well as political in my metaphorical meanderings. I thought about how rooted I have always felt here on the old homeplace. I never imagined, having such a powerful subconscious system holding me fast to the mountains, that I could feel at home anywhere else, but I had. During the year in Cuba, a new root system began burrowing its way into the fertile island soil, into another "Old Place." The re-entry shock in coming back home made me realize that living in Cuba for an extended time not only generated these new roots, the experience was also something of an uprooting. The *ida y vuelta*, the going away and returning, shook my foundations, challenging many of my long-held assumptions and values and sense of identity.

This does not mean that I no longer belong here on the family land. After all, the locust lying there on the forest floor still belongs to the

Old Place. Like the old tree, I am simply feeling more prostrate than upright these days. The locust had to die and surrender to the ground in order to become fully part of the life of the land again. It will eventually re-enter the community of the soil, with new roots and shoots emerging from it. Given time, I imagine something similar happening to me. Some things have started to die, which is not such a bad thing, from a biblical perspective. Some core values and assumptions that inform my identity have begun to be uprooted, and they will have to be surrendered to the soil. Over time, I imagine I will feel myself again connected to the life of this land, and maybe even send down some new roots.

I have read that in old growth forests, the ancient trees have root systems that intertwine and grow together, so that many trees share one set of roots. That is what I hope might happen in the subterranean spaces of my soul, and in the cultural substrata of two very different peoples: two root systems growing together, becoming one, to nourish and support life above ground in two countries, with two cultures walking together.

The oft-repeated meme that our countries are only separated by ninety miles is really only an illusion; the separation is superficial. When you plumb the depths well below the ocean surface, you discover that our two lands, like all lands on earth, are connected. Part of my desire in writing this book is to describe a bit of the rooting and uprooting that is slowly leading me to see these connections. Who knows, in my fall to the earth I might catch a couple of readers along the way and take them down with me. In the meantime, I hope I can narrate some of the life, some of the hopes and dreams, that are emerging from the soils of our connected lands.

Introduction

I read the news today, oh boy...
–Lennon/McCartney

Today, America chooses to cut loose the shackles of the past so as to reach for a better future–for the Cuban people, for the American people, for our entire hemisphere, and for the world.
–President Obama, December 17, 2014 speech

Están tratando de meter La Habana en Guanabacoa.
(They are trying to squeeze Havana into Guanabacoa.)
–Cuban expression

On the day after the big announcement, finding a *Granma* (Cuba's daily newspaper) to read about the big news was a challenge, because people had quickly scarfed up all the copies for souvenirs. Well before it was printed, though, the news began trickling out. Midmorning on December 17, 2014, rumors of a prisoner exchange circulated. Something unusual between the U.S. and Cuba was reportedly in the works. Both Alan Gross, the U.S. citizen imprisoned in Cuba for five years on espionage charges, and the remaining three of the five "Cuban Heroes" imprisoned in the U.S. for fifteen years on the same charges, had been released and were returning to their respective homes, as were other lower profile political prisoners. Later in the day, even bigger news spread as people learned of the two administrations' secret negotiations designed to end their fifty-six-year-old Cold War, thanks in part to the intervention of Pope Francis (who happened to be celebrating his birthday on this day).

In the ensuing months since December 17, many articles have emerged in major publications and many news stories have aired across broadcast and cable television, all documenting aspects of Cuban life. The pieces are captivating and well-produced, but I have been disappointed in one respect: the stories typically center on Havana, the capital city that has suddenly started to charm, if not bewitch, so many people who are now eager to visit this metropolis seemingly frozen in time, before "everything changes." As accurate as the portrayals are, they only show one thin slice of Cuban life, the urban scene of the country's power center.

While we did spend some time in Havana, Kim and I got to know many other urban and rural communities in eleven of the sixteen Cuban provinces, where we worshipped in twenty-seven churches and ate home-cooked meals in fifty homes. We were astounded by the incredible range of cultural diversity we found along the way. A "typical Cuban," or a "Cuban identity," is as hard to pin down as our own here in the U.S. What made the year fascinating for us was in part the timing, being there in the midst of the major narrative unfolding, seeing how people in different communities reacted to the prospects of a new day for our countries. For me, though, even more fascinating than this large public narrative was the impact of the thousand private stories of everyday Cubans, small but compelling stories of human resilience and creativity, humor and pathos.

Having a thousand stories is no exaggeration. Every day presented adventure after adventure, new thing after new thing, and ever deepening friendships, but this created a problem for me in trying to convey the experience. How can I fit a thousand diverse stories into one book? The challenge is similar to that voiced in the Cuban movie, *Bretón es un Bebé*: "How does one tell the history of a country whose history is far larger than its size?" For me, the question is, how does one tell the stories of a year that casts a shadow far longer than its length? Both the big story, on the grand scale of world history, and the many miniature stories, on the smaller scale of personal histories, assures that this year will occupy a space in my memory that will indeed be far longer than its calendar length.

The solution to my challenge came to me as I re-read my diary from the year and came across a conversation with my Matanzas friend Luis Ruiz. He is a sixty-something Bohemian, an aging hippie if you will, a poet, a philosopher, which is to say, often unemployed. He is tall, gaunt, with thinning hair, missing teeth, several days' growth of beard, and threadbare clothes. He is a great conversationalist, although I admit that I often had a hard time understanding the gravelly vocalization of his Spanish, caused by a lifetime of cigarette smoke irritating his vocal cords. Occasionally, when my friend and neighbor Orestes was part of one of these long conversations with Luis, I would debrief with Orestes afterwards. I would communicate to him what I thought I had understood Luis to be saying, to see how close I was. I felt successful if I was in the 50% range. Luis was one of the regulars I often ran into on the street, and he was always ready to sit in a café and converse over a cup of coffee. His two favorite subjects were Howard Zinn's revised history of the United States, and the Beatles.

I doubt many Cubans know who Howard Zinn is, but love for the Beatles is close to universal. The love affair got off to a shaky start, as the music was forbidden fruit, outlawed by Fidel Castro early on in the Revolution. He deemed it to be bad bourgeois influence, but his ban backfired. The prohibition predictably made the music even more popular. After Fidel Castro removed the prohibition during the 1990s, citing the ban as one of the "errors of the Revolution," he went so far as to commission a respected Cuban artist to create a sculpture of John Lennon. Once this iconic figure was firmly seated on his park bench, complete with 24-7 guards to prevent vandalism, the once furtive fans poured into the light of day.

Today you can find Beatles nightclubs and bars in virtually every major city, from Havana to Holguín. I met enthusiasts everywhere I went (there are scores of entries in my diary having to do with Beatles-related encounters). Of all the fans, none was more knowledgeable nor more fanatical in their love for the Fab Four than Luis. He speaks no English, but he has phonetically memorized practically all the songs. One night, during a sing-along Beatles concert at a park along the Río San Juan, someone stood and proclaimed Luis to be one of Cuba's great poets, and asked if he would recite one of his works. He complied, reciting from memory a long poem which I did not understand during the performance. I discovered its brilliance the next day when he brought me a copy of it. The title was "Eleanor Rigby: The Back Story" and the poet had invented and imagined this tragic lyrical figure's life before we pick it up in the song.

Luis Ruiz, Orestes Roca, and Stan Dotson singing Beatles songs in a Matanzas park, photo by Wanda Hernández

Along with knowing the lyrics, Luis also knows the back story (real, not imagined), of all the Beatles' albums and songs. So there we were one scorching hot afternoon, taking advantage of some air conditioning in the Café Atenas, and on that day it was music, not Howard Zinn, on Luis' mind. He began telling me all about the Sgt. Pepper album, how completely revolutionary it was, technologically speaking. He lost me in his enthusiasm for the technical details of producer George Martin's genius and recording engineer Ken Townsend's wizardry, something about syncing multiple reels to get around the limitations of tracks.

Luis reeled me back in when he started rhapsodizing over the lyrics, extolling McCartney and Lennon's genius in always being able to *meter La Habana en Guanabacoa*, a common Cuban expression used to describe the attempt to squeeze a lot into a small space. Luis used the song *A Day in the Life* as an example: *Look at how much material they put in there*, he said. *You've got those bits from McCartney's daily childhood routine, a tragic car-crash death, a film featuring Lennon in a lead role, war, potholes in a London neighborhood, all that and more. A day in the life, all right. All in four minutes.*

That gave me my image, my solution. Take a year's worth of stories, and *meter La Habana en Guanabacoa*. I'm no Lennon or McCartney, so I cannot get it all into a four-minute song, but maybe I can squeeze a good deal into twenty-four hours. My idea is to try and narrate as many stories as I can into a "typical" *day in the life*, through the lens of a particular day that turned out to be anything but typical. Starting with midnight, each hour will frame a chapter featuring aspects of daily life experienced during that time.

To highlight some of the vast cultural diversity that exists east of Havana, I will narrate these twenty-four sets of stories from the two communities I know best, where I spent the most time: Matanzas and La Vallita. The former is a decent sized city of maybe 150,000, a couple of hours from Havana, while the latter is a sparsely populated rural village in the central province of Camagüey, roughly ten hours by bus from the capital. Sharing stories of a day in the life as experienced by residents of each of these communities will highlight some of the things that bind them together, as well as some of the colorful contrasts in the Cuban culture. Hopefully there will also be some glimpses of our own culture and our shared humanity within their stories. And maybe, just maybe, the stories will shackle us to hope, to the possibilities of a better future, even as we become unshackled from our painful past.

Part One

Screen Time, Sexuality, and Sweet Dreams

12 midnight - 5:00 A.M.

Chapter One

12:00 Midnight – The News

and though the news was rather sad...
–Lennon/McCartney

Change is hard–in our own lives, and in the lives of nations.
–President Obama, December 17, 2014

Es un arroz con mango.
(It's all messed up. Literally: *It is rice with mango.*)
–Cuban expression

In some ways, the eclectic western Cuban city of Matanzas (known as the *Athens of Cuba* for its historical contributions to the artistic and literary life of the country) and the small central Cuban village of La Vallita (whose name means *cockfighting ring*) are worlds apart. In other ways, they are both solidly Cuban, with one of the solidifying factors that unites them being their shared experience of screen time, i.e., television watching. With only five stations to choose from: two educational channels, two entertainment channels, and a sports channel, the populations in each community are likely to be familiar with and conversant around the same programming. The five-channel selection is actually an expansion. In the early years of the Revolution, television was primarily a vehicle for the government to promote the ideals and values of its Triumph, with many hours of speeches by iconic leader Fidel Castro on the air at any given time. Over the years government propaganda began sharing space with soccer, soap operas, and a smattering of U.S. television fare.

Screen time is one of those clear contrasts that distinguishes our two cultures. As a demonstration of the premium the U.S. places on liberty, our citizenry has full freedom of choice of what to watch. We have hundreds of cable or satellite channels at our fingertips (let's see, do I want to see the HVQ infomercial on that new pressure cooker or the ESPN-2 arm-wrestling tournament or the *Modern Family* marathon or *South Park* or the C-SPAN coverage of redistricting legislation or...), not to mention the ready accessibility of just about any episode of any program that has ever been broadcast, always available with streaming on demand. Cuba's revolutionary ideology tempers liberty with other ideals, such as equality and social justice, limiting the freedom of television choice to those five channels: *Cubavisión, Canal Educativo, Canal Educativo 2, TeleRebelde,* and *Multivisión*. These stations serve as threads weaving together the lives of communities both urban and rural in the crocodile-shaped island, from the snout (East), to the belly (Central), and the tail (West).

La Vallita, located in the crocodile's belly region, is literally "off the beaten path," with its dirt roads heading off in various directions from the Carretera Central, Cuba's central highway that spans the length of the island. Our getting to La Vallita always involved a bus departing from the Matanzas bus station between 7:00 and 8:00 in the evening. The buses heading in either direction to transport people from one end of the country to the other always traveled through the night, as a strategy to beat the heat. Since there is not a bus station in the village of La Vallita, we always had to let the driver know ahead of time that we wanted to disembark there, between the scheduled stops in Ciego de Avila and Camagüey, and he would simply pull the bus off the side of the highway and let us off.

When in La Vallita we stayed in the home of Sila Reyna and José "Cheo" Cervantes and their family. We had visited there enough times over the years to know the way to the humble but very accommodating dwelling: turn on the dirt road by the *Hogar de Ancianos* (old folks home), walk five minutes and take the first right (another dirt road), and the house is another two or three-minute walk, on the left. No matter how much we tried to convince the family that we knew the way, Cheo would always be there on the side of the carretera to meet us, to help carry the bags, and to lead us home. We especially appreciated his presence and leadership when it was a cloudy night, because La Vallita without moonlight is about as pitch dark as it gets. While Kim and I would be prone to get sidetracked and meander around in the dark, Cheo could make his way home with his eyes closed.

Even at 3:00 or 4:00 in the morning, as soon as Cheo got us to the door and announced our arrival, a greeting committee would quickly rise to welcome us: Sila, Anabel (their thirty-something daughter), and Anabel's daughters, Rut Vivian, age eleven, and Lisy, age three. I suspect that Anabel was the only one who did not suffer greatly from that late night intrusion. She, like many Cubans I know, is a night owl. It is a mystery to me when she does sleep, because she is also an early riser, getting up with the chickens to brush Rut Vivian's thick black hair and help her get ready for school. She then makes her way to the carretera to hitch a ride to the slaughterhouse about fifteen kilometers down the highway, where she and her fellow butchers handle hundreds of chickens and pigs each day and prepare them for the markets.

Anabel Cervantes Reyna

Anabel, who is a lovely, sunny-dispositioned, full-figured woman with the same thick black hair as her daughter's, does not look like she belongs in a slaughterhouse. Having said that, I realize the sexism at play in such a statement, as I do not really know what a person who "belongs" in the line of slaughterhouse work would look like. I have heard enough stories of Anabel's challenges in the workplace to know that my sexism is not unique. She suffers greatly from the machismo culture present in the male-dominated world of butchers. More than once, though, I have witnessed the display of her professional skill on an unfortunate backyard fowl, and it is impressive.

After putting in a full day, she hitchhikes back home, has her afternoon bath, and helps prepare the evening meal. All this without the benefit of running water. Until this past year, the family got its water from a hand-pumped well in the back yard, but this source went dry sometime during the year-long drought suffered across the island. Now Cheo makes several trips a day across the road to a neighbor's well, where he hand-pumps five-gallon buckets and brings them back to the house to fill several smaller buckets: one for drinking, one for use in the kitchen in preparing food and washing dishes, and two in the bathroom, one for flushing and one for bathing and washing hands.

José "Cheo" Cervantes Garcia, photo by Anabel Cervantes Reyna

Cheo is short in stature and lean, strong as an ox, with a mustache and who-knows-what manner of hairstyle, as he is rarely seen without a ball-cap. He, like his daughter, works in agriculture, at a nearby cooperative farm. They both take great pride in being part of the food system that nourishes their community and surrounding communities. Cheo, also like Anabel, is a night owl. While Sila goes to bed with the girls at what I would call a decent hour to help them fall asleep, Cheo and Anabel remain in the sitting room in front of their relic of a television set, a fifteen-inch Russian model that needs fairly constant adjusting to bring in a good signal.

While I was not in La Vallita in mid-December, I can well imagine from my experience that as the clock struck midnight on the 17th, these two would have been unwinding from the day with some screen time. Cheo would have stayed up through *Noticiero del Cierre,* the closing news, a midnight summary of the day's headlines on the Cubavisión channel. The formula for Cuba's state-sponsored news broadcasts is fairly consistent and predictable: national news focuses on patriotic events (which are many), health care (extolling achievements such as the Cuban medical brigade's work in Africa fighting Ebola), and agriculture (explaining new technologies and celebrating the harvests of farms that meet production quotas).

World news generally converges on violent crime, of which there is always a steady supply of source material. The midnight report on the 17th would have recapped the tragic world affairs of the previous day, starting with the horrific massacre of one hundred thirty-two Pakistani school children at the hands of the Taliban. Also headlining the day was the end of a hostage crisis in Australia, with two of the hostages killed, and an update on the trial of a U.S. Marine, Joseph Pemberton, in the Philippines. Pemberton was charged with the murder of Jennifer Laude. He allegedly broke her neck and drowned her in a hotel toilet after discovering she was transgender. In Mexico, new questions emerged about federal police complicity in the disappearance of forty-three college students in the state of Guerrero. (The seminary students where we taught had organized a candlelight vigil not too long before this day to pray for these students and to protest the injustices being perpetrated by the Mexican government on its people. Celso, a student from Mexico, led the vigil).

The news would culminate with the broadcasters turning their attention to a wrap-up of the day's news from Cuba's northern nemesis. It was more than a bit depressing to watch coverage of our nation's news, as it was always bad. Here are some U.S. headlines *Noticiero del Cierre* would have highlighted in the midnight wrap-up of the events of December 16: The Supreme Court upheld the right of police officers to conduct illegal searches and seizures based on wrongful interpretations or ignorance of the law. In Oakland, twenty-five people were arrested in mass protests over police killings of unarmed African Americans. Cleveland Browns' player Andrew Hawkins was vocal in defending the growing T-shirt protest movement against police violence. Congress passed a new law requiring states to report police killings. Shooting victims of the Sandy Hook massacre sued makers of the assault rifle. A new immigration detention center opened in Texas, the largest of its kind, and the private company running it, Corrections Corporation of America, was in litigation for its maltreatment of immigrant children. Finally, in Pennsylvania, police continued searching for Iraqi War veteran Bradley Stone, who remained at large after killing his ex-wife and five of her relatives. A day in the life of the U.S. news cycle. Cheo would have gone to bed after taking it all in, leaving Anabel to see what Cubavisión was featuring as the late-night movie.

People in Matanzas would have also been soaking in the shocking news reports. Matanzas, unlike La Vallita, *is* "on the beaten path." Situated on the northern coast about an hour and a half east of Havana, there are actually two beaten paths to choose from to get there from the capital: inland on the Carerra Central, or the more scenic trek on the Via Blanca, which runs along the coast. Throngs of tourists make their way on this latter route and come through Matanzas on their way to nearby Varadero, arguably the most beautiful resort beach in the Caribbean, if not in the world. The only reason to take the inland route is to avoid traffic, or to visit or pick up someone along the way.

On Calle Medio, the main street of Matanzas, just a block away from the town square and Liberty Park, our friend Alberto was awake at midnight, viewing the same recap of news that Cheo and Anabel were watching as the calendar turned to December 17. Alberto is a night custodian for Centro Kairós, the community center connected to the Baptist church, where we made our home much of the year. He is in his fifties, tall and medium built, with a shaven head that gives him the look of Mr. Clean from the Proctor and Gamble commercials, if he only had the hoop earring. Alberto is employed by the Center to be a presence for security and assistance whenever they have guests staying in their dormitory-style hostel, which is often. As pleasant a person as you would ever want to meet, he is well-suited for the job.

I would occasionally make my way down the two flights of spiral stairs from our apartment and share some screen time with Alberto, as the television was his primary company for the night. Late night descents usually meant I needed to fill up our drinking water jugs from the Living Water filtered system, or turn on the pump to fill up the rooftop reservoir so we would have running water in the bathroom. While on my errand, I would stop and check in with Alberto. We would talk sports, music (he and his spouse Mimi had a great soundtrack of instrumental Beatles music playing in the background when we went to their house for dinner), and he would ask me about life in the mountains. Whenever the nightly news wrap-up was on, we would talk news.

It is interesting to see how people in Cuba react to the daily news as broadcast on CubaVisión. There are some similarities, such as the way people whistle through their teeth and shake their heads in disbelief at the level of violence in the wider world. *Ay Dios mío.* They also voice gratitude for not having to deal with such horrors in the Cuban society, where gun violence is virtually nonexistent.

I did notice a difference in the reactions between communities closer to the capital, like Matanzas, and communities distant from the capital, like La Vallita. The closer to the power center, the more cynical people seemed to be. I would notice people rolling their eyes at a broadcast touting government successes (often the reality of the good news had not "trickled down" to the people), with some people even mastering good impersonations of the regular TV announcers, mocking them in satire. The farther east we traveled, I saw and heard less cynicism. Likewise, when it came to world news, while there was not any doubting of the veracity of the events presented, there was a sense expressed among the more jaded

Matanzas viewers that the government's broadcasters were selectively choosing their news items. They suspected that all was not so bad in the wider world, not even in the enemy of the North, but that the state-run Cuban television would never have permission to tell any good news.

After viewing the news for a year through different lenses, I am not sure that the state-controlled media of Cuba are any more controlled or selective than all of our U.S. options that compete and shout at each other across the ideological spectrum. Cuba only had one slant, to be sure, but it also covered a lot more of the world's news than our talking heads do. When is the last time any of our news outlets had an economic segment informing us about the Brazil-Russia-India-China-South Africa economic block (BRICS), which gets a lot of press in Cuba? If Presidents Obama and Castro had not had a historic public greeting in Panama, how much coverage would the Summit of the Americas have gotten? These Summits are well covered in Cuba. There were many stories from around the world that are outside the scope of our media's interests, so they are not broadcast here. We have our own criteria for selecting what to air.

Such selectivity notwithstanding, be it here or there, when it came to the reports of massive violence, stories that are covered in both lands, it does strike me that this is one of the profoundly sad dynamics distinguishing the U.S. from Cuba. In our entire eleven months in Matanzas, this city of 150,000 people, I only heard of one armed robbery (and it happened at the little corner store right across the street from the church and community center where we lived). It was the talk of the town, being such an unusual event, and for some it was a harbinger of things to come (guns) when our cultures do enjoy more open exchange.

Some days after that robbery, when I had occasion to be on the internet (an infrequent occasion), I checked to see if there had been any armed robberies in my smaller hometown of Asheville, NC, population 87,000. There had been not one but *five* such holdups of convenience stores during the week of the Matanzas incident. That is a perfect illustration of *arroz con mango*, a truly messed up situation. Yes, indeed, *the news is rather sad...*

Chapter Two

1:00 A.M. – Commercials

He didn't notice.
–Lennon/McCartney

Change is even harder when we carry the heavy weight of history on our shoulders.
–President Obama, December 17, 2014

Mira...
(Look...)
–Cuban expression, interjection

After the closing news, as Cheo turned in for the night, Anabel (along with Alberto and other night owls) would have watched a bit of Cuban history, as this is what airs between the various programs, such as the news and the late-night movie. A bit of Spanish: the word for *news* in Spanish is *noticias*, i.e., notices. In the *New Oxford American Dictionary*, one of the definitions of *notice* is *a small advertisement*. Imagine a year free of advertisements. Imagine a year of commercial-free television. That proved to be one of the most obvious contrasts we experienced, and if we did not "notice" it much when we were there, it hit us like a ton of Madison Avenue bricks when we returned home and felt the inundation of commercials and ads. Little yellow minions were everywhere we turned, in the grocery stores, fast food joints, at gas station pumps.

It used to be in our televised culture that there was simply a series of station breaks interrupting programming, designed to create the desire to buy things, hence the moniker "soap opera" for the operatic dramas that peddled Palmolive and Prell and Proctor and Gamble products. The commercials I grew up with did their job; they worked their way into our psyches. We fool ourselves into thinking that we don't notice, that commercials are the time for a bathroom break or a snack run to the kitchen. They know how to say *mira,* and we look. I think about how easy it is to remember the slogans. if you are middle age or older you can test yourself and see how many of these bring products to mind:

Try it, you'll like it. Anticipation. You deserve a break today. The real thing. They're gr-r-reat! As much fun to make as it is to eat. Betcha can't eat just one. Magically delicious. M'm good, m'm good. Uncommonly good. We bring good things to life. I can't believe I ate the whole thing. I go cuckoo. Silly rabbit. Melts in your mouth, not in your hands. Finger lickin' good. How many licks does it take? Takes a licking and keeps on ticking. Sometimes you feel like a nut, sometimes you don't. Have it your way. You got your peanut butter in my chocolate. Double your pleasure, double your fun. Ask any mermaid you happen to see. Sorry Charlie! It's not nice to fool Mother Nature. Celebrate the moments of your life. Fill it to the rim. Good to the last drop. The best part of waking up. Plop plop fizz fizz. How do you spell relief? I'd rather fight than switch. Why don't you pick me up and smoke me sometime? I'd walk a mile. Let your fingers do the walking. You're in good hands. Take it off, take it all off. It pays to discover. Just do it. Where's the beef? My bologna has a first name. The quicker picker upper. It keeps going and going and going. Strong enough for a man, but made for a woman. Manly, yes, but women like it too. My wife—I think I'll keep her. You've come a long way, baby.

Like the Energizer bunny, U.S. advertising just keeps going and going. As effective as these notices were in my coming-of-age period of history, the ad producers did not rest on their laurels. They have been hard at work ever since, continually honing their craft. At some point the marketing geniuses started seeing their craft in terms of short films. Halftime commercials of the Super Bowl became more captivating than the game itself. At some other point, subliminal seduction gave way to product placement ads. At still another point, the Saturday morning cartoons and Pixar films became little more than marketing tools for Toys R Us and Walmart. Which leads to the current state of advertising, where we do not know if the vast array of toys and clothes paraphernalia are part of the propaganda promoting the movie, or if the movies are simply full-length promotions for the paraphernalia. We do know; it is both. Capitalism at its finest, making us all minions of Madison Avenue.

Being away from that avalanche of marketing was, to make use of one of the old ads, a very definite way to spell *relief*. I suspect it is impossible to know how much we are shaped by these ads until we are away from them long enough to at least notice they are not there. I would be remiss, though, in giving the impression that Cuban television is completely commercial-free. Just as our ads are placed to sell something, the Cuban government, which controls the airwaves, has something to sell, too. It is constantly selling the Triumph of the Revolution. Government officials are marketing their own version of manifest destiny, their particular rendering of history. While Cuban broadcasts do not have corporate commercials, they do interrupt their programming. These short interruptions air as five- to fifteen-minute documentaries of the people and events that make up Cuban history, from the nineteenth century wars for independence through the 1950s Revolution. It is like having short History Channel episodes sprinkled throughout the regular programs.

Many Cubans yawn and stretch during these short history bits. They have seen them and heard them countless times. They are paying as much attention as we do to the Ford truck commercial after the thousandth viewing. I, unlike the Cubans, found these ads fascinating. Watching them was one of my best ways to learn some of the important names and places from Cuban history. Many of the pieces serve to commemorate something or someone on that particular day: a battle, a hero, an event in one of the wars or the struggle to eliminate banditry, or the literacy campaign, or the health brigade. Like a calendar of Cuban saints, every day has something historic to commemorate.

Going back to my early immersion in U.S. network television, it reminds me of the Andy Griffith Show, an episode called "Alcohol and Old Lace," where two elderly sisters, Jennifer and Clarabell, sold homemade "elixir" on the side to Otis Campbell and his drinking buddies. The sisters had high morals, though, and would only sell their wares if it was a holiday, when there was a special occasion to celebrate. So the imbibers had to be creative and find things to commemorate, such as the day Sir Walter Raleigh's expedition landed on our coast, or Muhammad's birthday (*I had no idea there were so many Moslems in Mayberry*, Jennifer confessed to her sister Clarabell).

At any rate, the Revolution's marketers are every bit as creative as Otis Campbell in coming up with something to observe and commemorate on a daily basis. It was from these documentary shorts that I learned a lot about the life of Frank País, (a Baptist, the son of a Baptist preacher), who founded the July 26 Movement, one of the most important components of the clandestine war against the dictator Fulgencio Batista in the mid-1950s. Members of the First Baptist Church of Santiago de Cuba even composed a hymn in his memory, after he was gunned down in cold blood on the streets of the city in 1957. Frank País is now the face of Cuba's newly printed 200-peso bill.

I also learned about Henry Reeve, the young U.S. doctor who came to Cuba to help fight in the country's third War of Independence against Spain, and who died in the cause. Fidel Castro honored Reeve in 2007, naming Cuba's famous medical brigade after him, the brigade that assists countries around the world after disasters or in times of pandemic. The Henry Reeve Brigade was nominated for this year's Nobel Peace Prize, in recognition of these many years of heroic effort, including this past year's work in Africa combatting Ebola.

I also saw several short pieces celebrating the literacy campaign of 1961 (the year of my birth). As I was coming into the world, many thousands of Cuban children and youth were going out into their world, having been trained to teach people in every rural village and urban barrio of the country how to read. Sila Reyna, our host in La Vallita and pastor of our partner church there, was a part of this effort when she was 12 years old. The valiant effort gained fame by virtually eradicating illiteracy in one year. Cuba still gets requests from developing countries to send people to replicate the program. Sila gets emotional telling the stories of her experience, particularly of teaching her grandparents to read.

Sila Reyna Cervantes

I learned not to expect the same reaction to historical events that Sila displayed when reminiscing about the literacy campaign. I was teaching my course on leadership in the seminary, and the students showed great interest in a video produced by the Fellowship of Reconciliation. The video consisted of thirty-minute episodes documenting various social justice movements around the world, highlighting ordinary people who defied great odds to create change. I decided to add another video to the course, one about the 1961 literacy campaign, a short documentary called *Maestra*. I found it very moving. My students, however, had very different reactions from the enthusiasm they had displayed upon viewing documentaries of the Civil Rights movement, the anti-apartheid movement, the Danish resistance to the Nazis, and the Polish solidarity movement. Midway through *Maestra*, I could see that they were bored. When I asked them what they thought of the film, they said it was old news. They had been shown similar documentaries all their lives. They demonstrated and described what I would call *ad fatigue*.

This somewhat jaded, at times bored, reaction to the exhaustive and exhausting historical notices was not universal. Even in the western, urban centers where dissent is more concentrated, you can find people who take great pride in the stories. However, the cynicism was definitely more noticeable in places like Matanzas, and the pride much more prevalent in places like La Vallita.

I remember a time in Sila's living room, when her granddaughter Rut Vivian and her best friend Karina were playing or drawing pictures, waiting for the time when their favorite cartoon would come on. The television was on, but no one was paying attention. It was one of the between programming notices, this time about an occasion when the president of the World Health Organization had paid Cuba a visit to laud its health care system. Raúl Castro opened the event with a short speech, but before he spoke, the *Bayamesa*, Cuba's national anthem, was played. On hearing the opening lines of music, the girls jumped to attention, saluted, and sang along. I joined them, out of respect, and then talked to them about the anthem, asking if they sang it at school. They did, as part of the early morning routine.

I asked the girls about what else they do in that routine to start the day. I had heard about how the students stand and recite something about Che Guevara, the iconic Revolutionary hero. I asked what it was they said. The girls recited the line with great enthusiasm: *Pioneros del comunismo, seremos como el Che.* (Pioneers of communism, we will be like Che.) Herein lies another difference between these girls and some of their counterparts in Matanzas: people in the city told me about how sarcasm often gets injected into the schoolyard recitation. At times some of those who are exhausted by the propaganda will say: *We are like Che* and then whisper to one another: *we are suffocating, we can't breathe here.* (Che Guevara suffered from chronic asthma.) Or some of the older students might say, *We are like Che* and whisper *we abuse our spouses* (another of the hero's shortcomings).

I have no idea what percentage of U.S. citizens fully embraced the *Minions* phenomenon, munching on minionized Twinkies and wearing the promotional T-shirts and enjoying the movie, versus what percentage quickly became worn out by the overkill and who rolled their eyes at every appearance of the little yellow characters. Neither do I have any idea how many Cuban citizens fully embrace the propaganda of the Revolution and believe wholeheartedly in the project to perfect socialism, versus how many roll their eyes at it, as if it were their version of a minion's phenomenon. Some might even appreciate that image, given that the *New Oxford American Dictionary* defines *minion* as *a follower or underling of a powerful person*.

Perhaps Che and Frank País and Henry Reeve and the youngsters in the literacy brigade and the president of the World Health Organization have all been unwittingly transformed into minions of Fidel and Raúl, serving to promote the Triumph, masterfully marketing its achievements. All I know is that both ends of this spectrum–embrace and dissent–exist in Cuba, and my observation is that there are people all along the spectrum, with various feelings and reactions to the historical narratives woven into every station break. Whatever their reactions, one thing is certain to me: Cubans as a rule cannot help but be far more attuned to history than our citizens. They have lived and breathed the promotion nonstop for more than fifty years. The *notices* have worked their way into the national psyche, making Cubans a people of history, whether they like it or not. They do have the weight of history on their shoulders.

After a year without our version of commercials, I have a sense that we would be better off here in U.S. television land if the ad moguls were to promote a bit more of our history, allowing our own calendar of saints to interrupt regular programming, instead of convincing us what device we cannot do without. On December 17, we could have been viewing a short piece about the Wright Brothers and their first flight at Kitty Hawk, which happened on this date. On July 13, we could learn a bit about Walter Raleigh's ship landing on the Outer Banks. We may not be ready for the *People's History* of Howard Zinn, but even these tidbits would be a refreshing break from the world of commerce.

Chapter Three

2:00 A.M. – Movies

I saw a film today, oh boy...
—Lennon/McCartney

Rising at 2 a.m., Senator Patrick Leahy traveled to Andrews Air Force Base in Maryland. He passed through a gate between two heavily armed guards and circled around a building to where one of President Obama's backup planes awaited. Once in the air, Leahy sat at a conference table with the plane's other occupants, including Alan Gross's wife, Judy, and he reflected on the efforts that had brought them to that point.
—USA Today, December 17, 2014

A ver.
(Let's see.)
—Cuban expression

I do not know what kind of weather the travelers had for their momentous takeoff from Andrews Air Force Base, but Cubans were enjoying a calm, cloudless night on December 17, with just a sliver of new moon. On such a night, at 2:00 a.m., the little village of La Vallita is one of the best places for stargazing you can imagine. On this night, like other nights, the light of the stars would have been joined by the faint flickering of light coming from the very few houses which have a television.

I failed to note in my journal what late night movie was featured on Cubavisión that particular night, but whatever it was, it would have been competing with a rebroadcast of *Dos Caras*, the popular Brazilian soap opera, on Multivisión. I chuckle when I think of how Sila received criticism from some neighbors who are members of a fundamentalist church, because she and the family regularly watch the soaps. Sila had a great comeback, explaining how they would watch the family intrigue and observe the lack of integrity in the patriarch of the family, and the viewing often led to very good dialogue about biblical ethics and mandates. For example, they had had an in-depth family reflection considering what the mandate to "honor your father" would mean for the *Dos Caras* family.

For a different reason than that of the fundamentalist neighbor, I shy away from watching the Brazilian soaps. It is the difficulty of understanding the overdubbing of Spanish over Portuguese. I learned from trying to watch shows like *Dos Caras* how much I rely on lip-reading, as well as on hearing, when conversing in Spanish. That is why telephone calls are so difficult, and why the late-night movie is always my preference over the foreign novelas. The thing I do understand about this particular novela is from its title, *Two Faces.* As you might guess, the plot derives from the two-faced nature of the main characters. It brings to my mind the two faces, the *dos caras,* of Cuban culture: the communist party loyalist and the dissenter dreaming of democracy.

It is far too simplistic to limit the faces of Cuban society to these two, however, as there are multiple nuances and shades of each. The multiple personalities of Cubans do include the militant idealists and the disgruntled realists, but in between there are also various shades of pragmatism. These are the folks who do not have much energy or interest in the ideological wars, but they understand how to play the game or work the system to get things done.

I remember one Cuban, a delegate to the *Poder Popular* (People Power, their local government), saying simply that politics was all about getting street lights in your neighborhood. Pragmatists like this know how to use all the right words of revolutionary struggle, but only as a tool, to gain access to the resources and people who might help solve problems or improve their neighborhoods. Pragmatists tend not to complain. The dissenters would argue that they do not have the right to complain. We heard several people tell the story of a famous Cuban comedian who visited the States and was interviewed on television by a Cuban exile who asked him how life was in Castro's Cuba. His perfect reply: *I can't complain.*

Unlike me, Sila and Cheo and Anabel and the girls do not complain about the overdubbing of *Dos Caras.* They have no difficulty understanding the dialogue of the popular telenovela, and like most fans, they would have already watched the latest episode in its earlier prime-time slot. So at 2:00 in the morning Anabel always opted for the movie. Appropriately enough, the one Cubavisión late-night movie I do remember watching with her in La Vallita was *Before I Go to Sleep,* a badly reviewed psychological thriller with Nicole Kidman and Colin Firth.

I found that Cuban television tends to broadcast a fair share of badly reviewed U.S. films, always with Spanish subtitles. In this one, Kidman plays a woman who had suffered a brain injury some ten years earlier, causing her to have a peculiar type of amnesia. Each morning, she wakes up with no memory of anything that has happened in the past ten years, including what caused her injury. Firth plays her "husband" (spoiler alert), who each morning has to calm her down, tell her who he is, and explain what happened to her. He has placed sticky notes all over the house reminding her of significant things in her life, in hopes that something will trigger her memory. Without completely spoiling the movie, suffice it to say that at some point Kidman and the audience rightfully suspect they are not getting the whole story, and there is a major plot twist revealing that the movie has been playing with her (and the audience's) mind.

I thought as I watched it that this is yet another fitting image for the dissenters in Cuba: the daily government propaganda is like having sticky notes placed all over your walls, constantly reminding you who you are, but eventually you begin suspecting that you are not getting the whole story. Cuban dissenters are not the only ones with suspicions about the stories they are being told. U.S. historians like Howard Zinn throw plot twists into our own history all the time, arguing that the sanitized versions of U.S. and world history coming out of the Texas curriculum schoolbooks are little more than propaganda designed to brainwash an amnesiac citizenry.

Back to the movies. There is a reason for devoting an hour (a chapter) of the book to movie-watching, beyond the curiosity of what Cubans watch. It is all about conversation. Movies and television shows are favorite topics of conversations, both in places like Matanzas and La Vallita. When people ask what we did during our eleven months in Cuba, I could rattle off plenty of activities, like teaching courses, leading workshops, facilitating retreats, playing music, etc. Or I could say I spent lots of time sitting around talking to people. This is what drives some visitors crazy, those who travel to Cuba on mission trips expecting to "do something" like build a church or lead a backyard Bible club or repair a storm-damaged home.

At least in the church partnerships we are involved in, those constructive activities, as worthy as they are, are rarely found on an itinerary. The purpose of the partnerships is relationship-building, over the long haul. Which probably will lead to various projects, eventually, but the projects emerge out of the relationships, and are approached mutually, not in the old model of resource-rich church sending people and stuff to resource-poor church.

The new model is about discovering what each side's resources are, as well as each side's needs, with contributions of various kinds flowing both ways. That's in the long run. In the short run, the goal is developing friendships. In Cuba, such friendships evolve much the way they do in the U.S., through talking. This is a good motivation for U.S. travelers to learn Spanish! An old joke unfortunately has too much truth in it: What do you call a person who speaks two languages? *Bilingual.* What about three languages? *Trilingual.* What about only one language? *U.S. citizen* (apologies to all the Hispanic-American and Asian-American citizens and others who defy this stereotype).

Aside from sharing jokes, what is the topic of these conversations? Much like in the U.S., the talk often centers on screen time. Movies. TV shows. This hit me on my return home, when I visited with friends and found out how far out of the loop I was, as the conversations were around *Orange Is the New Black* and *Transparent* and *Jane the Virgin.* I was lost, not having seen any of the water cooler conversation shows. I have some catching up to do, but find myself still gravitating toward the Spanish-language shows I can stream on my IPad at the gym, the Telemundo novelas that have become something of an addiction. I justify the habit, though, as tuning in to *La Reina del Sur* or *Dueños del Paraíso* is the best method I have found for honing my Spanish.

So, back in Cuba, we did our fair share of talking about the latest movies showing up on Cuban television (movie theaters are few and far between). The movies air on Saturday and Sunday afternoons and late-nights throughout the week. If you do go to Cuba and want to practice your Spanish, asking people about their favorite movie or favorite genre of movies is a great way to get the conversation going. Everybody has a favorite, with the possible exception of our friend Tamara. I truly believe she has seen them all and she loves them all.

Tamara lives in the Versalles neighborhood of Matanzas with her spouse Lázaro, an artist and musician and prison chaplain. She laughs about her frustration in trying to watch a movie with Lázaro. He is always asleep within five minutes, unless it is a Samurai movie. He has a large collection of old black and white Japanese Samurai movies, and can brilliantly weave in a story from one of these films into any Bible study or devotion for the prison chaplaincy training he helps facilitate. Lázaro, deceptively thin and unassuming, is a black belt in Aikido. He is convinced that his martial arts training helped him survive the extreme challenges of his adolescent and youth years of the 1980s and Cuba's *Período Especial,* the Special Period of the 1990s, when the Soviet Union fell and the Cuban economy collapsed.

Back in La Vallita, Sila and Cheo's son, Amaury, shares Lázaro's love for martial arts films. Amaury, 30 years old, is married to Norma, and they have two wonderful children, daughter Nailen (13) and son Norly (3). Like his father and sister and many others in La Vallita, Amaury works in agriculture. For many years he labored on a dairy farm, manually milking around twenty to thirty cows every morning, building forearms that would give Popeye a run for his money. Now Amaury works on a factory farm, raising the pigs that will eventually make their way to Anabel's workplace before *this little piggy* finally goes to market. Underneath his physical strength is a very tender heart.

Some years ago Amaury learned of an elderly couple on the outskirts of the village who were attacked by thieves. Their goats were stolen, depriving them of their livelihood. Amaury saw to it that their herd was replaced, and he rode his bicycle to their home every day after milking, preparing their daily meal and getting their farm back in working order, until they could get back on their feet. From these two jobs, one official and one volunteer, he would head home and unwind, playing with the kids, eating dinner, and then watching one of the Bruce Lee movies he had recorded. He especially loved a documentary on Bruce Lee's life, and found many connections between the actor's Buddhist philosophy and his own Christian faith.

Amaury Pujol Reyna with his children Nailen and Norly and spouse Norma Días Cervantes

In Matanzas, we found our neighbors Orestes and Wanda to be avid movie buffs. Wanda, the most energetic and charismatic person I have ever met (just being around her wears me out!), loves both Cuban and foreign films. She names *Life Is Beautiful* as her favorite movie (she has a wide variety among her favorites, but this one stands out). This is not surprising, for Wanda has an eye for life's beauty in every context, be it tragic or triumphant. With flowing blond hair and a sparkling smile to match her eyes, she is herself a beautiful artisan with talent in many genres. She gets it honestly. Her father, Manuel, is one of Cuba's most beloved artists. Known for his paintings of peasant life and his ceramic work, he is also one of the *Granma's* political cartoonists, which he confesses can be a challenge in Cuba.

Wanda is Managing Director of the Kairos Center, a role which no doubt creates constant frustration, because the artist in her would rather have her hands in paint or a ball of clay or cutting up magazines for a collage. I tried, with only partial success, to convince her that she could see her leadership of the Center staff as an art, a place to invest her creative urge. As good as that sounds, there is just no comparing staff meetings or grant-writing to sculpting clay and splashing paint on a canvas.

Wanda Hernández Murga and Orestes Roca Santana,
photo by Nancy Bradley

Wanda's spouse, Orestes, pastor of the First Baptist Church in Matanzas, is a tall, thin, wannabe rock and roll star with the thick black hair of a rocker and matching soul patch. In another life, instead of pastoring his flock and deciphering Greek and New Testament as seminary professor, he could well be wailing out some undecipherable vocals on a stadium stage, fronting a heavy metal band. I consider myself something of a classic rock aficionado, but Orestes beats me hands down with his knowledge of 1970s rock trivia. A student of the English language via rock and roll lyrics, he once asked me to clear up a confusing line he did not understand: *What does it mean, a deadhead sticker on a Cadillac?*

Orestes has a good collection of rock and roll movies that demonstrates the breadth of his interests. We enjoyed watching documentaries of Lynyrd Skynrd, Metallica and an all-star concert homage to the Stratocaster guitar. In the latter, I was excited to know some trivia that Orestes did not, as I pointed out my hometown music hero Warren Haynes on stage, and proceeded to narrate story after story of the blues great's early career in Asheville.

Orestes shares with Wanda the wide variety of favorite films. He loves all Monty Python movies, with an ability to quote *Holy Grail* dialogue at length. He also loves the foreign films that are regularly featured on late-night TV. *Círculo*, a Bosnian war film, is a good example. He is also partial to *cine cubano*, and can recommend a long list of Cuban films for people wanting some exposure to the culture. *Conducta* is his latest suggestion.

It is interesting that the government censors have given, if not completely free reign, a long leash to the Cuban film industry. From the very beginning of the Revolution the movies have been (unlike the strictly controlled television programming) one avenue of criticism in a country where the revolutionaries have little patience for their critics. The classics of the early 1960s include biting satirical spoofs of the new government. A good example is *La Muerte de Un Burócrata* (Death of a Bureaucrat) by famous Cuban director Tomás Gutiérrez Alea. It totally lampooned the ineptness of government workers and the layers of bureaucracy of a revolutionary regime that had come to power with promises of putting an end to such bourgeois bureaucracy. Not that you would see these movies in a Cuban theater, but they are allowed to be made, and are readily available on DVD or thumb drive for people who want them.

Orestes and Wanda use some of the more contemporary Cuban films, like *Suite Habana* or *Conducta*, as resources for orienting groups visiting the church and the Center. Among other favorites are the more cutting-edge and hard-hitting critical satires from the dissenting director Eduardo Del Llano, who writes and directs an underground series of shorts spoofing life in Castro's Cuba, featuring the character Nicanor O'Donnell.

A brilliant full-length satire from Del Llano is *The Truth About G2*. What appears in the first part of the movie to be a scathing exposé of G2, Cuba's secretive security apparatus akin to the KGB or CIA, turns out to be about another "G2," a duo of Cuban rock and roll guitar wizards. Watching this with Orestes required clicking pause on the remote every thirty seconds, so he could explain the double-meanings of all the dialogue. What makes G2 and Nicanor and other Del Llano films interesting is that he is a Cuban citizen, apparently free to speak his mind through the medium of film. His expatriate counterparts in Miami would lead us to believe that anyone speaking out so strongly is destined to be a political prisoner. Del Llano contradicts those assumptions.

What the Miami Cubans would be correct in saying is that none of the Nicanor films, nor *The Truth About G2*, will show up on Cubavisión as the late-night feature. Here you will not find many Cuban films at all, unless it is an approved documentary about the life of Fidel or Che. However, in a relatively radical shift in censorship, Cuban television now airs a weekly satirical prime-time comedy that voices relatively direct criticism of the state of affairs in Cuba, poking fun at the utopian claims of the regime.

Until a few years ago, this kind of lampooning would have been unthinkable, given the severe limitations on any form of speech not supportive of the Revolution. The show is called *Vivir del Cuento*, which translates as *Living by the Story*, the "story" (*cuento*) in this case being understood as a fib, a lie. A *cuentero* is a teller of tall tales, and in whispered tones some people may even dare to tell you that Fidel is one of the world's great *cuenteros* with his propaganda of the wonderful life enjoyed by Cubans. *Vivir del Cuento* is quite popular, with its popularity rising the closer you get to Havana, where it is set. The show regularly serves up material for water cooler conversation, of the *it's funny because it's true* variety.

Late-night Cuban television, by contrast, will not offer up much in the way of such self-satire. It will give you plenty of foreign film fare, good ones such as *The Green Bicycle* (from Saudi Arabia), or stinkers like *Little White Lies* (from France). It will also give you a good smattering of Hollywood. José Martí, Cuba's "Apostle of Independence," famously said that he was living in "the monster" while he was in exile in the U.S. for a time before the war in the late nineteenth century. To underscore Martí's point, a good percentage of the Hollywood movies shown in Cuba will be in the horror and monster movie categories.

There are notable exceptions. Among them are movies starring Anabel's favorite actor, Danny Glover. While I had to confess to her that I had only seen a small handful of his nearly one hundred movies, she could rattle off movie after movie of his. We had more than a few long conversations about these movies, the ones I knew (*The Witness*, *The Color Purple*, *Beloved*), and others she introduced me to (*Death at a Funeral*, *2012*, *Lonesome Dove*). Oddly enough, in one of those conversations, we both had a brain freeze. Neither of us could remember to save our lives the title of his most famous set of movies, where he pairs up time and again with Bruce Willis in a buddy cop series. One afternoon some days later, watching her butcher a back yard chicken for supper, I had the *ah ha* moment and out of the blue yelled out "Lethal Weapon!" Her butcher knife must have jogged the title out of my memory bank. We were both relieved to have that out of the way.

Anabel Cervantes Reyna with a tool of her trade.

Anabel also enlightened me on Danny Glover's Cuba connection. In 2011 he had traveled to Havana as a UNICEF Goodwill Ambassador, and there he received the Tomás Gutiérrez Alea International Cinema Award by the Association of Cuban Writers and Artists. Glover was a strong advocate for the release of the Cuban Five, even visiting one of the heroes in prison. He also had a starring role in a 2010 documentary, *Will the Real Terrorist Please Stand Up?* which probably contributed to his receiving the award. An amusing bit from the film has Glover on the streets of Los Angeles with a camera operator, interviewing random people:

> Danny Glover: *Excuse me, sir. Do you know who the Cuban Five are?*
> Man on Street 1: *Weren't they those guys that played the U.S. in the semifinals of the Pan American Games in the basketball tournament?*
> Man on Street 2: *Oh, yeah. Aren't they that salsa band?*
> Man on Street 3: *Americans?*
> Danny Glover: *No, they're Cuban.*
> Man on Street 2: *Why haven't I ever heard about that?*
> Woman on Street 1: *The Cuban Five? They're that rock band, right?*

I did not know it at the time, but I later learned that Catherine Murphy, director/producer of *Maestra*, the documentary about the 1961 literacy campaign in which Anabel's mother had participated, was also one of the producers of this Danny Glover documentary. She and I had exchanged emails when I was trying to get a copy of *Maestra* to bring to Cuba. It is a small world, indeed. Something else to add to the conversation next time I am in Anabel's living room in front of the flickering TV.

Chapter Four

3:00 A.M. – Sexuality

I'd love to turn you on.
–Lennon/McCartney

If someone asked me "what is happiness?" I would say it is what we are living in Cuba at the moment, with the return of our heroes to Cuban soil, welcomed with all the deep and sincere affection of all our very committed people. It really is difficult to describe what we are feeling. I'm going crazy wanting to get out to the street with the Cuban flag as students are doing to celebrate this moment.
–Mariela Castro Espín, December 17, 2014

¡Candela!
(hot, edgy, sexy, in a party mood)
–Cuban interjection

The day I started writing this chapter, another stark Cuba-U.S. contrast came across social media. Two owners of a progressive, hip coffee shop in my town were outed as having posted some terribly misogynist commentary in blogs and podcasts on a supposedly "anonymous" website. Scores of unhappy people went to the streets of West Asheville to protest what these baristas had been broadcasting, their boasts of alleged sexual exploits, including a rape of a woman under sedation at a hospital. The "outing" exposed for many of us just how much of this kind of sick and twisted sexual violence exists on social media.

I have long warned my Cuban friends who are eager for their island to become fully wired, so that everyone can have full access to the internet, to be careful what they wish for. I shudder to think about how quickly the worst threads from the World Wide Web, such as these "angry men" or hard-core porn sites, will capture Cuban youth. Such technological hopes and fears, however, are the subject of another chapter. This one is about sexuality in Cuba.

I want to make a confession and a disclaimer. First the confession: I am by nature a modest person, not particularly comfortable with much public discussion (online or otherwise) of private matters. It does not take me long to get to the "TMI" (too much information) moments of a conversation. Which leads to the disclaimer: This chapter, while focusing on the topic of sexuality in Cuba, is not going to be the Cuban *Kama Sutra*. I am not going to presume to know what is going on in bedrooms or other private spaces at 3:00 in the morning. I took to heart the euphemism my parents always used when referring to genitalia: they are one's *privates*, so don't expect me to invade anyone's privacy.

That said, the 3:00 a.m. chapter is as good as any to approach the topic, especially given the lack of privacy in the majority of Cuban homes. One of the symptoms of economic ills in Cuba is the housing shortage, which means that over half of Cuban homes are sheltering three or four generations under one roof, often in very tight quarters, with beds sometimes separated only by a makeshift curtain. Couples seeking to "couple," if they have anything like my modesty toward matters private, would want to wait until the nearby parents or grandparents or children or grandchildren are safely snoring in deep REM sleep before engaging in intimacy.

In *Bailando*, an ear-worm song we heard everywhere we went throughout the year, Decemer Bueno and Enrique Iglesias rhapsodize a lover's dream: *quiero estar contigo, bailar contigo, vivir contigo, tener contigo una noche loca* (*I want to be with you, dance with you, live with you, have a crazy night with you*). In the cramped quarter Cuban context, the sexual fantasy of the extremely popular song really does sound like a fantastical pipe dream—enjoying a full night of crazy loving. One hour in the middle of the night is probably the most anyone can realistically expect.

Cramped styles notwithstanding, sex is a hot topic of conversation in Cuba. Maybe part of the sensuality is due to it being a hot-climate island, where people wear less clothing and lack the Victorian morality generated by cold-climate England. Or it might have something to do with the Latino culture, which involves a lot more touching, hugging, and kissing in casual encounters. Whatever the causes, there is a palpable sense of pent-up sexual energy at work there. A compelling scene in the movie Suite Habana shows the image of pressure cookers venting steam, juxtaposed with a miniskirt-clad young woman walking down a busy street, eliciting a different variety of steam from the onlookers.

Inside that kitchen pressure cooker would be a variety of seasonings to flavor up the black beans, cut of pork, or caldosa (Cuba's national soup). Likewise, inside the metaphorical pressure cooker a variety of seasonings—distinct global influences, body images, gender constructions, government codified ethics, and spiritual traditions—are giving a particular Cuban flavor to the main dish of *eros*. These "ingredients" form the outline of my reflections for the chapter.

To begin with, whatever can be defined as authentically *Cuban* in any cultural sense, including areas of sexuality, has to take into account a wide range of global influences throughout the course of the island's history. The pressure cooker of Cuba is something of an exotic-erotic melting pot in this sense, with understandings of gender and family and courtship coming from west Africa, Spain, France, Holland, England, China, Korea, the United States and Canada, the neighboring Caribbean islands, and Russia, to name some of the primary people groups who have had a significant presence in Cuban history. In terms of sexuality, Jamaica is the latest to stir it up, as Cuba's contemporary pop music is dominated by the genre "reggaeton," a Jamaican-style rap music similar to much of North American hip hop in its focus on sexual themes.

Hearing first names reveals the global influence as well. Along with plenty of Cubans named Carlos and Francisco and Lázaro, our acquaintances include a man named Kim (with Korean heritage), Kimbo (leader of an African-based religious community), Juan Pierre, and Vladimir. When Multivisión aired a late-night documentary explaining how Russians historically survived the bitter north cold, it provoked plenty of jokes based on what people had learned about the Russians' sexual practices.

Within that melting pot, however, probably the strongest influence around sexuality has to do with the culture of *machismo*. This strong understanding of fixed gender roles has double roots, with both Spanish and African varieties contributing to the powerful and dominating male ego. In areas of the island where the African influence is strongest, such as in Bayamo on the eastern end, boys are taught from a very early age to be proud of their plumbing fixtures. Toddler boys typically run around and play in the nude, or with only a shirt, and are taught to show off what they have. Girls do not, by contrast, have the freedom to boast or show off their plumbing.

In terms of the African influence on women, the Yoruba spiritual traditions have a pantheon of deities that does include a powerful female presence, Oshun, the goddess of beauty, love, and fertility. Perhaps this accounts for the strong female ego of Cuban women that somewhat counteracts or balances the machismo. When we attended an interfaith cultural event in the Marina, one of the neighborhoods of Matanzas where Afro-Cuban religions are prevalent, women were definitely in charge.

Within all this exotic-erotic mixture of sexual energy and tradition, one dynamic does provide a contrast with North American family values: ethnic and racial mixing is much more the norm all across the island. Interracial couples do not seem to be drawing on the same kind of "jungle fever" that Spike Lee documented in his film. I cannot say when the crossing of this barrier first started in Cuba, but it apparently has been happening long enough to have become normative. Every church we visited, across the theological spectrum, had a decent percentage of interracial couples.

On the surface, this would lead visitors to believe that racism does not exist in Cuba, but it does, only in subtler ways. Because of the hubris of Havana, much of the prejudice in Cuba is directed against people from the opposite end of the island, and by chance, the Eastern provinces are where the African influence has historically been the strongest. As the global economic crisis hit Cuba, causing many people from the east of the island to migrate west in search of employment, Havana residents began referring to these migrants as "Palestinians." So while black-white couples are commonplace, a *Habanero-Palestino* pairing might just raise some eyebrows.

Moving from the global to the personal, a second pressure cooker ingredient that seasons the stew of Cuban sexuality has to do with body image. More than a few times, U.S. women visiting Cuba have been taken aback by the "compliment" they received from Cuban women. *¡Ay, que gorda parece!* "My, how fat you look!" or "Wow, you've fattened up since you were here last!" In La Vallita, Sila Reyna asked me one time what she had said to offend a woman whose countenance had fallen after the introductory meeting and salutations, and I explained to her the cult of thinness that captivates our culture. Sila, herself a bit *gorda*, found such an outlook baffling. As a diabetic, she does have to watch her diet, which is difficult to do in Cuba, given their narrow range of culinary choices, but she had never encountered the idea of dieting for looks, or the notion that being waif-like was the way to be attractive.

Behind Sila's lack of awareness is another of the stark contrasts with our culture: there are no magazine stands at the checkout line in the grocery or pharmacy. No *Cosmopolitan*, no *Maxim*, no *Fx*, no *Sports Illustrated* swimsuit edition. There are no *Ladies Home Journals* telling women how to lose weight so they can be more attractive (next to the recipe for the best strawberry chocolate pound cake). While there is bound to be an underground market for *Playboy*, there are no Seven-Elevens displaying it on their racks, nor do the vast majority of people have access to the internet's exhibitionism. As a result, they have come to construct their ideals of beauty on their own, in the absence of such marketing madness. Sila and Anabel are indeed both beautiful women, with none of the self-loathing that many in our culture sharing their body type would endure or battle.

On Calle Medio, the main business street in Matanzas, near the church, there is a storefront family business selling CDs, and Yosbel, the young proprietor, pipes his music onto the street pretty much nonstop during the business hours. Yosbel plays an interesting variety of Cuban and U.S. pop music. It always killed me that along with *Bailando*, one of the other songs regularly cycling through the mix was the old 1970s chestnut by the Commodores, *Brick House*. Having spent a good deal of time with groups of visitors walking along the sidewalks of Calle Medio, I can recount several conversations with people who would hear that song and remark that Cuban women are indeed attractive (in a physical as well as spiritual sense). It is true. However, not many of them are, as Lionel Richie celebrated in the song, *36-24-36 (what a winning hand)*.

I also remember a conversation with one of the teenage girls in the church, Ana María, about which nation could boast the most beautiful people. We were at the airport waiting to greet a group of Canadians. I argued that Cuba wins hands-down. She disagreed, claiming that, at least as far as she was concerned, the most *guapo*, the best looking boys, were from Canada (possibly because her long-distance boyfriend is Canadian). About the time she was making her argument, out the airport door came our group, led by two retired Canadian men sporting Hawaiian shirts with suspenders holding up Bermuda shorts, complete with knee socks and sandals. I milked that scene for a long time with Ana. *¡Guapo!*

Ana María Triana Mendoza, selfie photo

A more serious conversation around teenage girls and young women and body image has to do with eating disorders. Probably again due to the lack of media frenzy dictating what is sexy and attractive and what is not, I saw very little evidence of anorexia among Cubans. Of the hundreds of girls and women we saw in those eleven provinces, including many trips to various beaches, I can only think of two Cuban women I know who look unhealthily thin. Being skinny is as rare as being obese. I suspect that this is already changing in places like Havana where the North American influence is strongest, but at least for now, outside of Havana, being a bit *gorda* is the refreshing ideal. I laugh at the Cuban version of the "five-second rule" when food is dropped on the floor. Their saying as they blow off the dust and pop the fallen food into their mouth is *lo que no mata engorda*. That which does not kill you makes you fat. A good thing.

Along with social constructions of beauty, Cuba is undergoing a reconstruction of sorts when it comes to gender identification, a third seasoning for sexuality. Kim and I had the great blessing of auditing a class with Ofelia Ortega, one of Latin America's finest ethicists. It was on the Ethics of Gender, and one of the themes of the class was the difference between biology and sociology in defining gender. We addressed the conventional wisdom that what it means to be male or female is biological in nature (dealing with the physicality of one's privates), whereas what it means to be masculine or feminine is something every society constructs, and reconstructs over time. We talked about how emerging voices from the transgender community are challenging the dualism of that conventional nature-nurture way of thinking.

In Cuba, this ever-fluid concept of gender is another of those conversations that has taken place by way of films. A classic Cuban movie from the 1960s is *Lucia*, a film in three parts that examines what it was like to be a woman in three periods of the country's history: we see a nineteenth century colonial woman named Lucia, a 1920s Republic-era Lucia, and a 1960s Revolutionary Lucia. Another look at gender and sexuality comes in the 1990s celebrated film, *Fresas y Chocolate*, about Havana's gay subculture. A contemporary Cuban film we saw and discussed in class was *Cartas de Amor* (Love Letters), about a woman whose cottage industry was ghostwriting love letters for people. The movie looks at ten of the people who employed her, what their love situation was, and why they needed a love letter. Among the ten were two gay men, one of whom was a stereotypical "effeminate" artist, for whom you would not need much gay-dar to guess his sexual preference. The other was a surprise, a cowboy from the rodeo, whose willingness to be "outed" by the film took some courage, given the machismo culture of Cuba.

Ofelia Ortega talking with Sila Reyna and other seminarians

Some of our more enlightening conversations around gender did not come in the classroom or in front of a movie screen, but with our friends in the group SOMOS. Translated "We Are," SOMOS emerged out of the Matanzas First Baptist Church a few years ago as the first faith-based non-hetero-normative advocacy and alliance group in Cuba. The phrase "non-hetero-normative" came about, as I understand it, from the challenge of knowing which letters to put in the continually expanding list defining non-heterosexuals: lgbtqim... It became easier just to say *non-hetero-normative*.

SOMOS was inclusive enough, though, to give space for normative heterosexuals like me to join them as allies. While one Saturday night a month was closed to us hetero folks, the other three Saturdays were open (one-night dealing with various issues the community faces, one a Bible study, and one a social activity). The group loved it when I wore my "Honorary Lesbian" button, given to me by friends when I participated in their holy union service twenty-five years ago.

Cute jokes aside, I learned from this group just how sheltered and relatively traditional I have been in my thinking. A young Afro-Cuban named Lázaro Rivero brought the lesson home to me, when the group was discussing various gender constructions and where people felt they fit along the spectrum. Lázaro, muscular and tongue-pierced, said something reminiscent of punk rocker Patti Smith, who was promoted by her record company as "beyond gender," and who famously said, "as far as I'm concerned, being any gender is a drag." Lázaro said that he did not need any kind of sexual identity and refused to be pigeonholed into any category of gender. He simply loved the people he loved, and had fun with the people he wanted to have fun with. Maybe he was channeling Tom Jones as much as Patti Smith (interestingly enough, a Tom Jones concert was aired on Cubavisión as the alternative to the late night Multivisión documentary on the cold Russians). *It's not unusual to be loved by anyone. It's not unusual to have fun with anyone.* The "we are" of SOMOS provides a broad tent, indeed.

Lázaro Rivero, selfie photo

Such comments could be written off if they were simply overheard in the context of a fringe group's meeting. In Cuba, though, questions of gender are far from the fringe. They are front and center in the national spotlight, thanks to the fourth ingredient in the pressure cooker: the government's promotion of codified ethics related to gender and family issues. In recent years the subject has been highlighted by the advocacy work of none other than Mariela Castro. As her name implies, she is part of the "royal family," daughter of President Raúl Castro, *diputado* (delegate) to the People's Assembly (their version of Congress), and Director of Cuba's national Sex Education Center. She well could have been a serious contender to be the third Castro to head the government. She is definitely smart enough, and is quite charismatic in front of a crowd. Some say, though, that her devotion to the cause of civil rights for the non-heteronormative community has pushed her out of contention among the powerbrokers of Cuba's culturally conservative elite. Others say she has pushed herself out.

This next-generation Castro has the dubious distinction of casting only the second "no" vote in the history of the People's Assembly. Cuba's national government works on something of a consensus model. They presumably work out all their disagreements in committee, so that once a piece of proposed legislation reaches the floor, the expectation is unanimous passage. (Eat your heart out, Paul Ryan.) The first "no" vote came, I am proud to say, back in the 1990s from the first Christian leader elected to the Assembly. Raúl Suárez, retired pastor of Ebenezer Baptist in Marianao and founder of the Martin Luther King Center there, voted "no" because his conscience would not allow him to support capital punishment. He took some heat for his public dissent, but he has continued to win reelection and to serve.

Mariela Castro's "no" vote came as the body was proposing updates to the nation's *Código de Trabajo*, the workplace Code of Ethics. She had fought to get "gender identity" specifically listed among the categories of workplace rights and protections, along with race, class, sexuality, etc. The final legislation that made it to the floor for the vote left out the transgender community, so she cast her lonely but loud "no" vote.

This speaks to one of the differences between the sexual revolutions in our respective countries. In the U.S., the 1960s liberation movement was street-based and counter-government. In Cuba, the sexual and family revolutions are set squarely in the middle of government deliberations. Early on in the Revolution, Fidel Castro, prompted by the advocacy of brother Raúl's spouse, Vilma Espín, led the way in engineering both the Workplace Code of Ethics and the Family Code of Ethics (*Código de Familia*). Both aimed to bring equality, fairness, and justice to women.

Instead of lobbying the government for reforms, as in our country, the government there began its campaign to lobby the culture for reforms.

Mariela Castro Espín, talking with CENESEX lawyer Manuel Vásquez and Stan Dotson, photo by Elaine Saralegui

After fifty years, these codes are as familiar in the Cuban countryside as they are in the urban centers, as I learned from Sila. A couple of years ago she was visiting us in our home in North Carolina, and she exuberantly celebrated the way I took charge of washing dishes after dinner. *Un ejemplo del Código de Familia!* she cried out. An example of the Family Code! It was the first time I had heard of the *Código*, and asked her to explain. It is something that every couple has to agree to when they get married. They have to sign off on it. It essentially targets the husbands, telling them they have to share equally in all domestic duties, and not take advantage of the wives, who otherwise are likely to be saddled with three jobs–work outside the home, housework, and childcare.

To be sure, signing this document to get the marriage license, and fulfilling the pledge, are two different things. It is still a revolution in progress. In La Vallita, Sila often would repeat to spouse Cheo her excited discovery about my share of the domestic work, how I was a model of the Code. I doubt this reminding was done to prompt him to action, though, as Cheo was also a model of in-home cooperation. He always seemed willing and able to share in child-care, along with many of the home duties, taking care of the yard, bringing in the water, etc.

As a side note, I can speak directly to Mariela Castro's in-person charisma. I had the privilege of meeting her, thanks to my friend Elaine Saralegui, the founder and leader of SOMOS, who took me to a big-deal conference focused on the battle against homophobia in the workplace. It was a surreal experience, as I not only got to meet keynote speaker Mariela, I got to translate a conversation she had with Troy Perry, a U.S. visitor who back in the 1960s had founded the Metropolitan Community Church, the first church to open its doors to gay, lesbian and trans believers and seekers.

I stood there between the two, at first wondering how in the world this First Family member could get away with being so open and free to engage complete strangers in a public setting (no Secret Service-type bodyguards in sight). Then I began wondering what my elementary and high school teachers would have thought at such a preposterous scene (I was less than mediocre in both English and Spanish classes). That was all in the back of my mind. In the front of my mind, I was doing my best not to mangle either language too badly, while hoping that Elaine or someone in the group would snap a quick photo.

Luis Pérez Martinto

Another of our SOMOS friends had a far more consequential meeting with Mariela Castro. He is Luis Pérez Martinto (he insists on including his second family name, reminding us that he had a mother as well as a father). Luis, a bespectacled short man with short gray hair, speaks several languages and teaches French for a living. He has a sharp wit and a powerful story to tell, a story that captured the interest of Mariela when she heard him share it at another conference.

Luis was an adolescent when the Revolution triumphed, and he was victim of one of the admitted "errors of the Revolution" (dissenters are quick to note that there have been far more errors than those admitted). This "error" involved the new regime's treatment of homosexuals. They, along with criminals and religious leaders, were sent to UMAP, whose sanitized acronym relates to agricultural production, but it was in reality more of a forced labor camp. Luis would say it was a full-blown concentration camp, designed to "re-educate" or "re-wire" the people with "defective" world views inconsistent with the Revolution. Homosexuality was viewed as one such defect.

Luis had known from a very young age that he was gay, and his family accepted him and loved him with no questions or challenges to his identity. But as a young teenager, the government marched him off to UMAP, for what he describes as one of the most horrific periods of his life. He survived, in part (and this is what caught Mariela Castro's attention) because it was in UMAP that he first fell in love and had a boyfriend.

This relationship lasted beyond UMAP, but the man eventually left Cuba for the greener U.S. pastures. Luis continues to correspond with him as a friend. The story was compelling enough to Mariela that she convinced people at HBO, who were doing a documentary on the sexual revolution in Cuba, to interview Luis and include his story in their movie.

Along with Mariela Castro, another of the official state-supported "rock stars" of the sexual revolution that I had the pleasure of meeting is Patricia Arés, a psychologist and professor who makes regular appearances on Cuban television talk shows. She is something of the Doctor Ruth of Cuba, although her interests take her far more into the fields of child and family therapy. I mention her because she is an example of how the official party line of the government, from the beginning of the Triumph, has been that their Revolution is scientifically based. They have been trying to socially engineer a utopian society of justice based on research of both hard and soft sciences.

Dr. Arés understands that the traditional paradigms of family have been radically shifting (the marriage rate is, as it is in our culture and elsewhere, in sharp decline). Her research convinces her that the real culprit of trauma and mental illness, when it comes to issues of family and sexuality, is not the non-hetero-normative experience, but is the homophobia and machismo still woven into the traditional culture.

A final ingredient in the pressure cooker stew of sexuality involves the country's rich traditions of spirituality. As much as the government is in the driver's seat in the social engineering efforts of new sexual paradigms, I found the most riveting and captivating conversations to be in the church setting, in talks connecting sexuality and spirituality. As SOMOS was by design an open group that invited ecumenical, interfaith, and secular participation, there was a wide range of perspectives on these connections. Along with representatives of Catholic, Baptist, Presbyterian, and Episcopalian traditions, the group counted among its members a Santeria priest as well as people who professed no faith.

The monthly Bible studies, which started around 8:00 on a Saturday night, were absolutely the most engaging experiences of approaching scripture I have ever witnessed. I generally had to call it a night before the studies finished, as the group would still be in deep dialogue, popular education style, well past my bedtime. The topics varied, from ways the early church argued about and dealt with diversity, to cases of biblical civil disobedience around matters of family and sexuality, to the possibility that the Roman centurion's slave healed by Jesus was in fact an indentured sex worker, to the analysis of the Levitical prohibition of men lying with men "as with a woman" to be about ancient Near Eastern patriarchal honor and shame codes. According to these mores, to be penetrated sexually was to be dominated and shamed, i.e., *to be like a woman*, and no man should shame himself or another man with such inferiority that they likened as being natural to womanhood.

For me, even more fascinating than the Bible studies was the way this "fringe" group was challenging the "center," the assumed norms and values of the mainline church. I was long accustomed to language within mainline liberal churches of "welcoming and affirming." Elaine and others in the group let me know, though, that they were not that interested in the language of inclusion and all that it implies. For them, to be "included" in the mainstream still assumed that the mainstream has the power and the right to decide who is in and who is out. Instead of being included and welcomed, Elaine said they were more interested in challenging the church, questioning its core assumptions, and inviting it to leave its four walls and Sunday morning worship emphasis and be present out on the fringes where Jesus is, among the sex workers plying their trade for survival, the transgender folks rejected by family, the non-hetero-normative people harassed and abused by police.

These conversations, when they included representatives of the non-normative fringe and the normative center, were not and are not easy. It occurred to me that this conversation is an example of how the Church as "Body of Christ" has entered into a phase of history not unlike the developmental stage of puberty. The Body of Christ's pubescent voice is surely changing, as it talks about the connections between sexuality and spirituality. In addition, the Church today is fairly fixated on its "privates" (this seems to be true across the ideological spectrum), much like 12 and 13-year-olds are. As happens with pubescents, we are living through an awkward phase that is bound to involve much uncoordinated tripping and falling along the way, as the Church grows into its adult self.

Elaine Saralegui, photo by unknown

Occasionally there are some "graceful" moves in the awkward tripping among the normative folks. I heard a couple of the "straight" leaders of the Cuban church world acknowledging the prophetic and necessary role Elaine and SOMOS and people like them are playing. One was Reinerio Arce, who was Rector at the seminary during our time there (since retired from that position). He also happens to be married to psychologist Patricia Arés. At the same conference where his rock star spouse had presented, Reinerio used the parable of the Good Samaritan to both bless and challenge the non-hetero-normative listeners. He said that the contemporary Church is in the ditch, having been beaten and robbed of its vitality by the culture of homophobia. It will not be the traditional priests and deacons of the Church who will rescue it, but the traditional pariahs, the gay, lesbian and trans believers. The Church desperately needs rescue and healing, Reinerio said, and he implored the fringe community to stay with the Church, not to pass it by, to care enough about this injured "body" to be its Good Samaritan.

Another straight leader in the Cuban church, our friend Samuel, who is a retired social worker and a Baptist deacon, held out an even more radical hope, that the non-hetero-normative community will lead the way in the human evolution of what we understand to be love, what we understand to be the role of sexual pleasure in loving relationships, and what we understand about God. Samuel is writing his own exposition of this theme, so I will refrain from stealing any more of his thunder.

I am not sure if Lennon and McCartney had any idea what their words, *I'd love to turn you on*, would be signifying in the twenty-first century Cuban context. At 3:00 in the morning on December 17, or on any given day, I have no idea what any of this that I have observed says about the privacy of what was happening or is happening between the Cuban sheets (more likely on top of the sheets, as it is too hot for covers), no matter who you are talking about: Orestes and his spouse Wanda, Sila and her spouse Cheo, Elaine and her girlfriend Yivi, or young Lázaro and his "anyone." *¡Candela!*

Chapter Five

4: 00 A.M. – Dreams

I went into a dream.
—Lennon/McCartney

A future of greater peace, security and democratic development is possible if we work together–not to maintain power, not to secure vested interests, but instead to advance the dreams of our citizens.
—President Obama, December 17, 2014

Que sueñes con los angelitos.
(May you dream with the angels.)
—Cuban goodnight wish

I began writing this chapter on the day after Pope Francis spoke to the youth of Cuba. Someone sent me a transcript of his talk, which he made after having had a private meeting with one young person. The Pope referred to this conversation, saying *a word hit me hard: "dream" . . . In the objectivity of life must come the ability to dream. Young people who are not capable of dreaming are closed in on themselves. Sure, you might sometimes dream things that never will happen. But dream of them, desire them, seek horizons, open yourselves, open yourselves to great things.*

I don't know if I would call it a great thing, but I recently found myself in the waiting room of a car repair shop, where I watched a rerun of *Castle*, which happens to be one of the U.S. dramas that airs in the wee hours of Cubavisión programming. I never stayed up to see it there, but this episode I ran across had the main character, novelist Richard Castle, feeling unsettled by a recurring dream. More like a nightmare, it was giving him clues about a suppressed memory of what had happened to him during the months he had gone "missing." While the plot was not all that compelling, I did resonate a bit with Castle, having gone "missing" myself for almost a year from familiar surroundings, and often experiencing the plague of recurring and unsettling dreams.

I tend to remember my dreams. For people like me who tend to go to bed early (around 10:00 or 11:00), the longest and most vivid dreams occur in the 4:00 hour, in the fourth or fifth cycle of REM sleep. As with movies, dreams can be a great conversation starter. *I had a crazy dream...* Many of my Cuban friends love to share their dreams, and some enjoy trying to help interpret those of others. It is not by accident that at the base of beloved Cuban artist José Villa Soberón's statue of John Lennon in the Havana park bearing his name (Lennon Park, not to be confused with Lenin Park, twenty-five minutes to the south), a marble tile reads *Dirás que soy un soñador pero no soy el único.* You may say that I'm a dreamer, but I'm not the only one.

Orestes Roca Santana, photo by Nancy Bradley

Our next-door neighbors for much of the year, Orestes and Wanda, dear friends who became as close as family, the younger brother and sister Kim and I never had, are among those dreamers, and we found them to be good dream interpreters as well. Their apartment bookshelf includes classics in the field of depth psychology and the archetypal symbology of dreaming. So it was great fun to be in their living room or on a long walk, when any one of us might bring up a puzzling dream in hopes of unraveling its mysteries. In one of Orestes' recurring dreams, he is on the streets of Matanzas, surrounded by a deafening silence. The city is completely void of people, but there are many churches dotting the landscape. At some point in the dream, he always glimpses one person emerging in the distance, crossing the street at an intersection on bicycle. There the dream ends.

One possible interpretation he had considered focused on the politics at play, with the depressing feeling that his decaying city had become a vast wasteland, and the presence of churches an absurdity, with no one needing ministry or being drawn to worship. I offered a different interpretation that I hope proved helpful to Orestes: I reminded him that he is deeply drawn to silence and contemplative prayer. It occurred to me that the dream was an example of the *apophatic* mystical tradition, the *via negativa*, which finds mysterious richness in the emptiness and silence of God's presence. Orestes could have been seeing himself on the bicycle, faithfully journeying through the silence, cycling though the emptiness.

We had a similar enriching conversation around another of his unsettling recurring dreams, where he is in the once glorious neighborhood of Versalles, and is surprised to find that the crumbling barrio has become filled with many big and elegant churches. Again, the dream seemed to be presenting symbols of sacred presence in a place many have given up on as a decaying shell of its old glory.

I had my own recurring nightmare throughout our eleven-month stay, one that would disturb my sleep at least once a week. I shared the dream with Wanda and Orestes on a long walk to his parents' home in the Pueblo Nuevo neighborhood, and I am really glad I did. As we crossed the Río San Juan and viewed the beginnings of what will be the city's pedestrian boulevard, I explained that while the details of the dream always differ, the context and theme are the same. The dream places me back at the college where I worked for a dozen years until I was fired at the end of a lengthy battle with the administration.

Always in this dream, I am back at the workplace, even though I know I have been fired. I am hanging around, not sure what to do, and always in the dream someone on campus finally delivers the message to me that I really do not belong there anymore. They question what I think I'm doing there. Trust me, in my waking hours over the years since the departure, I have done what I consider sufficient emotional work to process the failed windmill tilting adventure, eaten my crow, made my peace, learned my lessons, etc. My dreams, however, seemed to be telling me otherwise, and I could not for the life of me figure out why.

Before venturing into interpretation mode, Wanda asked questions about the back story, the history behind the dream. I filled her in on the long and (for me) sad saga, but instead of showing sympathy, her eyes brightened. She said they do not usually hear those kinds of stories from

North American visitors. We always come seeming to have our acts so together. So she was grateful for finally hearing a *fracaso*, a story of failure, a poorly resolved conflict among good, well-educated people of faith who presumably share core values. The story reassured her that Cubans are not the only ones who at times fail to live up to their beliefs and ideals, who fall short of the glory of their stated missions. The misery of my failure found some good company.

Then, she and Orestes eased into interpretation. I say *eased*, because instead of directly deciphering the dreams, what they did was ask me questions, questions I had not thought of, and their probing caused me to do some thinking, out of which an interpretation began to emerge. Their inquiry was not about the college, not about my specific role there or the conflict, but it was about the essence of what I had been doing in my work. Leadership development. Civic engagement. Empowerment. Whether they intended it or not, behind some of their questions, and the glint of smile in their eyes, I intuited that they were wondering if what our overachieving superpower nation really needed was more leadership and empowerment.

Through Wanda and Orestes' gentle but on-point questioning, I began to suspect that my dreams were telling me something far more profound than the surface issues of conflict and job loss. Maybe it was the very nature of that work, leadership development, that was not a home for me anymore, no matter what the context. This conversation and my reflections that followed helped me get a handle on why some of my students wanted to change the title of the course I was teaching: "Spiritual Practices of Leadership." They did not like the word "Leadership," and wanted to change it to something like "Encouragement" or "Facilitation" or "Collaboration." They felt their world had had enough of leadership.

Maybe the troubling dream was probing me to question how it is that we followers of Jesus, the One who calls us to a place of surrender and denial of self, can get so wrapped up in leadership and empowerment. The dream interpretation reminded me of a project I had done several years ago, interviewing pairs of people with similar vocations in the U.S. and Cuba: an artist, a pastor, a linguist, a clown, a musician, a doctor. I asked the same set of questions about their life's journey and calling. In doing a qualitative analysis of the interviews, an interesting finding emerged. Among the U.S. folks, no matter the career, issues of leadership development and capacity-building had arisen in the answers. Among the Cubans interviewed, no matter the career, a different concept kept popping up: *entrega*, surrender.

Maybe part of what I was learning from the Cubans was how to surrender, to let go, of assumptions, privileges, ambitions, who knows what. Maybe that is what the nightmare was trying to teach me, that my home is no longer in the context of *empowerment*, but in *entrega*, that I no longer belong in the world of development, but just the opposite. The emotional work of processing failure and job loss is not enough. There is spiritual work to undertake in processing a new foundational home base.

When I began to unearth these discoveries about the fundamental nature and relative value of the work I have done in my life, I had to laugh. Throughout the trimester at the seminary, while I was having my nightmares and teaching my course, I was doing research and writing a paper for a theology course I was auditing. The research was on the question of what is "good" work, focused on the thoughts of two Cuban theologians, the father and son team of Sergio and Reinerio Arce. It was as if there was this hidden but powerful conspiracy of grace working its way through my life, leading me away from one life's work and toward another, and I was finally getting it.

Speaking of grace, I had another grace-filled experience on the way home from our dinner with Orestes' parents (a fabulous feast, as always. His mom makes some of the best *mojito*–not the cocktail–but the oil and garlic topping for starchy vegetables). I shared another recent dream that had been troubling me. In the dream, my long-deceased father was still alive, and was showing me the trail to a bold spring we had gone to when I was a child, a special memory in this alternative dream world. He knew the hidden trail through the woods. When we got to where the spring was supposed to be, instead of flowing water we found it was where Kim and I had built our house, right on top of the spring. I felt so disappointed, and I could not figure out how I could have missed seeing the spring when building the house.

Orestes and Wanda both laughed heartily and jumped in with the same interpretation. No questioning this time. They said it was obvious, that we *are* the spring, that our lives are now the spring. Sure, there is a feeling of nostalgia, wishing we could return to the world of childhood with Daddy, but we are not in that world. We are in our world, and we have constructed our lives in a way that flows. We found the magic spot, and we were attracted to that spot because of its flow. Wow, I'll take that interpretation, which is a perfect demonstration of how this couple has such a powerful capacity to bless and affirm. Good neighbors, who became good family as well.

Some dreams need little interpretation, little help from Jung or Freud, as they can eerily mirror a real-life event. This happened with Sila, before she moved to La Vallita in the mid-1990s, in the throes of the Special Period. She and Cheo and their two very young children were living about an hour away, in another small pueblo, Piedrecitas (Little Rocks). If the despair brought on by the shortages of the 1990s was not enough, the family was going through its own special period of sorts, experiencing severe emotional stress, to the point that Sila was not sure that anything in her life was secure, neither her marriage, nor her housing situation.

In spite of all this, she was confident she was being called by God to pastor a church, to serve a community. She just did not have a clue as to how or where. Then she had a dream. It was of a humble community, dirt roads, no running water, and a small, simple house. That was it, a vision of a house. In the dream she heard a voice, a voice she had never heard before. She understood it to be the voice of God. It said, "Look, this is your house. This is where you will live." She woke up with the assurance that this community, this house, was where God wanted her. But she had no idea where it was located.

Sometime later, as she continued to pray for guidance as to where to go, her brother called to tell her he had been to the little village of La Vallita for some business, and had seen a house for sale there. He wanted to take her and show it to her. She went, and there before her very eyes was the very house from her dream, down to every detail. When the woman told her the price, 10,000 Cuban pesos ($400), Sila's countenance fell. She only had $200 and no prospects for getting the rest. The woman surprised Sila by telling her not to worry. She had a feeling that the house was supposed to be hers. She said she would take the 5,000 pesos, and trusted Sila to pay the rest when she could. Not long afterward, the President of the Fraternity of Baptists, Paco Rodés, visited Sila in her new home, and was excited about the prospects of a new Fraternity church in the area. He encouraged her, telling her not to worry about the money. Three days later, it arrived, and the home was hers, debt-free.

Despite having no furniture, Sila was rejoicing to be home. Slowly, the family stress eased, and she began forming relationships with her neighbors. She shared the gospel good news, and a church formed in her living room. Her spouse Cheo was the first to be baptized; later came the children. Sila is still in the home, now with grandchildren around her, and a small sanctuary built in the backyard for the congregation that outgrew her living room. It is all a dream come true for her.

Sila's dream is illustrative of one of the many contradictions I observed in Cuban culture. This type of spirituality, in which one experiences direct communication from God through dreams and visions, is generally associated in our culture with more conservative traditions of Christianity. Additionally, our culture usually sees conservative religion tied to conservative politics. Sila does not fit that mold. Those connections do not work for her. She has dreams and visions, direct from God, and whenever she is facing a situation without clear direction as to what to do, she will simply open up her Bible, and the page it opens to will provide her an answer. This is another practice often associated with conservative spirituality in our context.

When it comes to politics and social issues, though, she leans far to the left, as one of the most loyal supporters of the Revolution and its leadership that I have ever met. She has a thoroughgoing communitarian ethic based on love and social justice for everyone, no exceptions. It is a reminder that the dynamics of church and state are very different among Cubans, and our categories simply do not hold there.

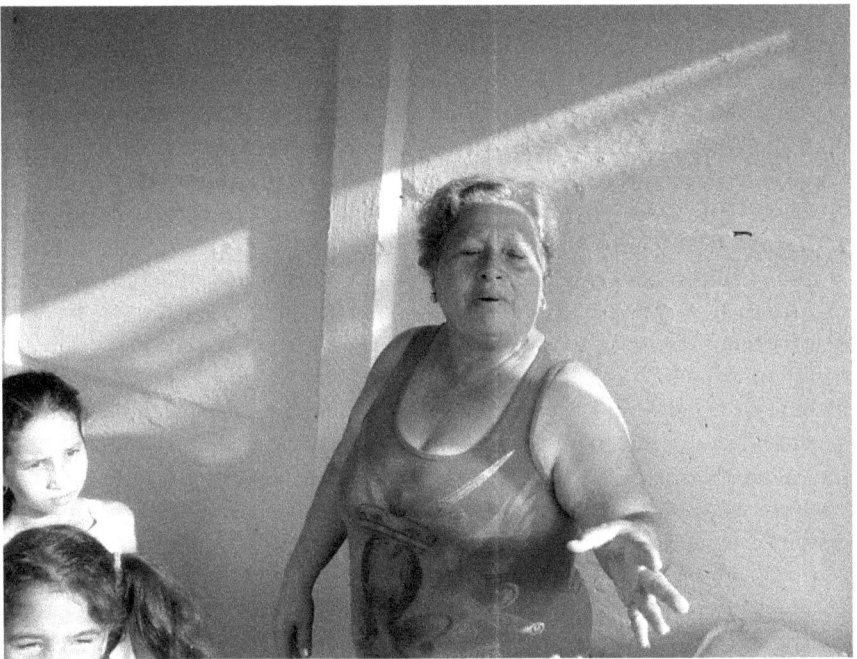

Sila Reyna Cervantes

Along with literal dreams and visions, the Cubans we met embodied José Martí's poem *I Dream Awake*, where he said, *Day and night I always dream with open eyes*. We enjoyed engaging our friends in conversations about what their open-eyed dreams were, both personally and for their country. I remember several years ago asking a group of young children in Piedrecitas, where Sila lived before moving to La Vallita, what their dreams were of their future, and they were all filled with ambition. A young boy dreamed of being a scientist, a young girl a dentist, another young girl a pastor, another boy a farmer.

This is one of the poorest communities I have been to in Cuba, with barely passable dirt roads and very few homes with running water, and yet their young people were filled with dreams and possibilities. I thought of how different this conversation would in the context of an impoverished community in the U.S., where hopelessness and despair reign and severe limits are placed on the futures of the young. By contrast, in Piedrecitas each of those children has been able to realize their dreams. The science teacher and dentist may not make enough money to live on, but they are able to follow their calling.

Not all the young people of Cuba are idealistic, though, especially in these days of scarcity. It is difficult to dream when you are struggling to make ends meet every month. I asked my seminary class one day to describe their dream for what Cuba would look like in twenty-five years, how their communities might be different. The students in this class of about a dozen, generally very engaged and talkative, met this particular question with a deafening silence. They had trouble imagining a different world.

Others among our Cuban friends do dare to dream, some in terms of personal development, others in terms of community or societal development. Brian Julio is a 20-something Matanzas actor who dreams of being on stage and screen in Havana. Our artist friend Lázaro in Matanzas dreams of engineering a water treatment system for his neighborhood in Versalles, to get the run-off water out of the streets. Sila's congregation in La Vallita dreams of developing a sustainable agriculture project in the back yards of members' homes. Rut Vivian and Nailen, Sila's granddaughters, dream of being *maestras* like their grandma. At 12 and 13, they already show obvious signs that they have the gift.

When people ask me about my year in Cuba, one of the standard questions I get is if I started to dream in Spanish. That is apparently one of those key benchmark indicators that signifies one is really learning a language. I answer "yes," but the way Spanish entered my dream world was kind of quirky. It generally happened in anxiety dreams, where I was frantically trying to conjugate verbs. I would reel off different verb tenses, usually in nonsensical ways. I am sure these dreams emerged because of a particular activity I had been facilitating in all sorts of contexts: the seminary course, youth retreats, chaplaincy workshops, etc. It was an interactive exercise that involved telling stories with three sets of action verbs, related to the three figures who appeared in the biblical story of the Mount of Transfiguration: Elijah, Moses, and Jesus.

I suggested to the students and workshop participants that one way to interpret the story is to see Elijah and Moses representing two traditional kinds of energy, that of fight and flight. In the Elijah story, the prophet calls down fire from heaven and slaughters all his rivals, the enemy prophets of Ba'al. This is the confrontational fire of *fight* energy. In the Moses story, a pillar of fire guides him and the liberated slaves as they flee from Egypt toward their land of promise. This is the liberating fire of *flight* energy. Fight and flight–these are two common human responses to crisis or conflict or challenge. The story gives us a third energy, though, as Jesus is transfigured by a third kind of fire, one that causes his face to shine like the sun and his clothes to radiate with brilliant light. He then descends the mountain to heal a young boy. This is the redeeming fire of *transformation*. It is the third way, an alternative to the fight or flight choice.

In the activity, we used these three stories to describe three very different dreams of Cuban people. The class or workshop participants would be divided by three, and each small group would take one of the stories and see how many verbs they could think of to narrate the story. For the Elijah story, there were verbs like fight, defeat, struggle, vanquish, battle. Then the group would use those same verbs to talk about Cuban culture and the dreams associated with those verbs. It was easy. The energy of *fight* has been ever present since the Revolution started, and fight verbs continue to be ever present in the propaganda slogans seen on billboards and wall graffiti. *Seguiremos en combate* (we will continue in combat), *venceremos* (we will vanquish), and the most famous, from Che's goodbye letter to Fidel on leaving for Bolivia, *hasta la victoria siempre* (onward to the victory, always).

The fight energy is seen in the church as well, as Cuban theologians foster a militant faith, reflected in some of the more popular hymns of the church. *Danos un corazón, grande para amar, fuerte para luchar.* Give us a heart, big to love, strong to struggle. *Andaremos por el mundo con fe y esperanza viva... luchando.* We walk through the world with faith and living hope... battling.

Depending on where various Cubans stand vis-à-vis the Revolution and the Party, they have distinct understandings of what it means to be at war. For some, it is combatting the one-party rule that has dominated the horizon and limited their political options for fifty-six years. For others, it is resisting the imperial threat of the United States. Mariela Castro exemplified the latter in an interview reflecting on the possible implications of the new diplomatic relations announced on December 17: *If the United States intends that these changes take Cuba back to capitalism and a return to being subservient to the hegemonic interests of economically powerful groups in the United States, they must be dreaming.*

The small group looking at the Moses story also had an easy time coming up with a long list of verbs: flee, escape, run away, move, emancipate, rescue, liberate. These verbs are very present in the dreams of many Cubans who are eager to escape their harsh reality. A U.S. Jewish news agency also reflected this dream of liberation in its announcement of the release of Alan Gross on December 17: *The release and return of Alan Gross from Cuban incarceration is truly a modern day Chanukah miracle, and it fills us with deep gratitude to, in the words of the Amidah, "He Who frees captives."* Mr. Gross' expedited liberation seemed a distant dream, and now it is a dream come true.

This flight energy is acutely felt in the story of Cuban emigration, both internally and externally. Internally, there is an ongoing exodus of people from east to west, toward the capital. The massive unemployment of the global economic crisis has led to this westward movement. Many habaneros are not welcoming of this influx. Eastern immigrants from places like Bayamo and Santiago and Holguín are disparagingly called "Palestinos." Some of the Easterners have embraced the name as a source of pride, in a quest for justice that binds them in some ways to the Palestinians. The larger exodus, though, is from Cuba to points north, to Miami or Canada or Spain. The country has been hemorrhaging young people since the 1990s, with first the Special Period and then the global economic crisis creating disillusionment with the utopian communist dream.

The third group's challenge was to come up with another set of verbs, alternatives to the fight or flight energies, representing another dream, a "third way" of transformation. Using the Jesus story, they came up with verbs like forgive, redeem, embrace, heal, cleanse, share, restore, inspire. Unlike the other two groups, though, this one found it really challenging to apply these verbs to the Cuban context. Stories of healing and forgiveness and redemption are not as common as those of fight and flight.

The beauty of the exercise came when they began to have *aha* moments in naming some of the ways their churches and faith leaders have embodied this third energy: creating the Martin Luther King Center in a marginalized neighborhood of Havana, founding the Kairos Center for the arts and liturgy during the Special Period in Matanzas, starting a nationwide prison chaplaincy program. The young pastors in the 1960s who made the decision to stay in the country and convince the Party that Christianity was not an enemy of Revolution, but could be its partner in serving the poor and giving hope to the hopeless, they are heroes of the dream of transformational energy. *Day and night,* they dream with their *apóstol,* Martí, *with open eyes.*

Sila Reyna in the little village of La Vallita is one of those awake open-eyed dreamers. Her ministry exemplifies the verbs *forgive, redeem, embrace, heal, cleanse, share, restore, inspire.* Sila is the one from whom I learned the ritual goodnight wish, *que sueñes con los angelitos.* She and her band of angels continue to dream the sweet utopian dream of a community that shares all things in common, bound together by the Gospel of love.

Part Two

Street Life, Soft Bread, and Sweet Café

5:00 A.M. - 10:00 A.M.

Chapter Six

5:00 A.M. – To the Bus Station

Woke up, fell out of bed, dragged a comb across my head.
–Lennon/McCartney

U.S. Representative Chris Van Hollen [Alan Gross' Congressional Representative] said he woke up early and arrived at Joint Base Andrews in time for a flight that departed at 5 a.m. The direct flight took three hours and ended at a smaller airport outside Havana–not the city's main international terminal, he said. Just a few minutes before landing, another U.S. plane landed carrying three Cuban nationals convicted of spying in 2001.
–Washington Post, December 17, 2014

¿Cómo anda?
(How's it going?)
–Cuban expression

The weather on December 17 was back to normal, high 77 and low 71, after our first "frente frío" (cold front) of the year had given us a couple of days of temperatures in the 50s, causing much shivering and scrambling for coats among the Cubans. I am not normally awake at five, and the few times I was up and about at that hour demonstrated that I am not alone in my sleeping habits. The streets were for the most part clear. An exception these days would be the presence of two aspiring pilgrims, Orestes and Lázaro, who are preparing for a walk on the Camino in Spain by rising at 5:00 on Mondays, Wednesdays, and Fridays, when they embark on a two-hour hike out of the city, followed by contemplative prayer and breakfast.

One of my rare early morning excursions happened when I walked to the bus station, located a couple of miles away from our apartment, in the Pueblo Nuevo barrio, south of downtown Matanzas, across the Río San Juan. It was a different time of year, late April, and already the complaints of *hay calor* (it's hot) were on everyone's lips, with temperatures reaching well into the 90s during the day and not coming down much at night.

I was going to meet Sila, who was making the long trip from La Vallita. Her eight-hour bus ride was scheduled to arrive at the Matanzas station around 5:30. The unusual light rainfall on my walk (we were there during a year of drought) offered me a much appreciated break from the heat. As I headed south on Calle Medio (Main Street), I saw no one except for an old man in tattered clothing, sweeping the streets and putting the garbage in his push cart, to take who knows where. I greeted him as I passed by, *¿Cómo está?* He responded with *¿Cómo anda?*

I smiled, as our exchange reminded me of the way my neighbor and soul sister Wanda and I had come to greet one another. It started when I told her the strange way my ear works in hearing Spanish. Whenever I was on the street and heard someone give the standard *¿Cómo anda?* greeting, I would look around for Wanda. My ear picked up *mo' Wanda*. She then shared how my name, *Stan*, is difficult for Cubans to pronounce. There are no words in Spanish that begin with *st*, so they have to throw a vowel in front *st* words. In Cuba I am *Están*, which happens to be the third person plural for the verb *estar*, to be. So whenever Wanda heard someone asking *how are they? (¿cómo están?)*, she looked around for me. Hence, instead of asking *¿Cómo está?* (how are you?), Wanda began greeting me with *¿Cómo están, Están?* (How are they, Stan?). My standard response came to be, *¿Cómo anda Wanda?* (How's it going, Wanda?)

After exchanging pleasantries with the street sweeper, I noted, as I often did in walking through Matanzas, that its street garbage was one of the unfortunate things that set it apart from almost every other city (except for Havana, which is also sanitation challenged). Sometime during the year I came up with a theory about the trashiness of Matanzas, which in all other respects is a lovely and attractive city. My theory was deemed as good as any by some of the locals. Western Cuba, which includes Matanzas and Havana, seems to contain more of the dissenting voice of Cuban life than does the central and eastern parts of the island. This dissent is the key to my theory.

At first I thought it was a difference between urban and rural, but I don't think that is it. I spent a decent amount of time traveling east, visiting friends in several of the bigger cities, and noticed two differences. One, people do not seem to be as caustic about the government. They generally seem more supportive of the Revolutionary regime, or at least have learned to play by its rules to get things done. I expected to find this in the rural villages, like La Vallita, where the elders still remember and narrate the miseries of rural life before the Revolution, and appreciate all it has afforded them, even with its mistakes. It also seems to be the case, though, among city folk, who in their conversations appeared to be more sympathetic of and at times downright proud of the Castros' long tenure of leadership. Western Cubans by contrast are much freer with their cynicism, if not direct criticism, of the regime and its propaganda.

The second observation: urbanites in the center and east of Cuba take pride in the cleanliness of their cities. This contrast did not go unnoticed by other matanceros traveling east. Whenever friends from Matanzas would go to a workshop or event somewhere east, almost all would come back remarking on how clean their destination city was. So here's the theory: if I am correct in my observation, if there really is more of a concentration of complaint and dissent in Matanzas, I can imagine the powers that be saying something like, *okay, complain all you want. You can stew in your own juice, or in your own garbage. We're not going to bend over backwards to keep your nest clean.*

Boy playing "street sweeper" in Matanzas

Another twist on the theory: Some agree with me that it is a case of people soiling their own nests, because if the city was doing a good job with its sanitation, then that would be proof of sorts that socialism works, and the dissenters do not want that. A point in favor of that theory comes in the absence of trash bins along the Matanzas streets. When I asked why you see trash bins on the streets of other cities but not Matanzas, I was told that sometime in the Special Period of the 1990s, that crisis time brought on by the fall of their primary economic benefactor, matanceros started stealing the street trash bins, for no good or useful reason (it was not like stealing bread).

All theories aside, there was this tattered old man at 5 A.M., homemade broom in hand, sweeping up the previous day's mess and hauling it away. As I passed St. Teresa Avenue I breathed in the delicious smell of the daily bread baking in the Aguila Bakery. With the bread in the oven, four or five of the bakers were taking a break from heat, smoking cigarettes in the drizzle. The end of Calle Medio brought me to the Vigía, a renowned handmade book shop, a tourist destination as well as the site of an international academic conference dedicated to this type of artesania. We learned the day after this conference that a professor from Wake Forest University, where Kim's dad worked for half a century, had been a presenter. We were bummed to have missed her.

The Vigía is located next to a tourist restaurant which is one of the few places in Cuba where I found French fries. Past the restaurant I approached the bridge that would take me over the San Juan, the river which separates downtown Matanzas from Pueblo Nuevo. The bridge is one of seventeen in Matanzas, crossing either the San Juan or Yumurí Rivers which empty into the Bay of Matanzas. These spans give the city one of its nicknames, The City of Bridges, and from this particular bridge you can look down along the San Juan and see Calle Río (appropriately named) blocked off. Another unique feature of Matanzas: it is the only major city in Cuba not to have the traditional Latin American pedestrian boulevard. After years of debate as to where to situate such a boulevard, they have begun construction on it there along the San Juan.

Bridge over Río San Juan in Matanzas

Cuba: A Day in the Life

Manuel Hernández

One feature of this riverfront walk will be an attraction that has been there for many years, the Lolo Galería-Taller, a wonderful workshop/studio/gallery. From the bridge you can see the entrance, with the twenty-foot-tall metal bird sculpture standing by the door, sporting fan blades for its plume and a wheel for its foot. The Lolo shop is a working studio and gallery for a group of avant-garde and traditional sculptors, painters, glassblowers and ceramic artists, including Manuel Hernández, who uses the Lolo gallery to display his signature series of paintings featuring a traditional Cuban peasant couple.

We had the great pleasure of getting to know Manuel by way of our friendship with Wanda, as he is her father. During our year there he was honored with the publication of a biography that debuted during Cuba's annual book fair. *Manuel = Manuel* is a collection of interviews that traces his artistic life from childhood in the countryside to present day. Kim and I first came across his work many years before we ever met him. We were in New York City touring various art museums, and someone suggested a visit to the United Nations. The U.N. lobby was featuring an art exhibition of political cartoons from around the world, all around the theme of war and peace, with one artist from each U.N. member country contributing a piece. One of our favorites was the piece from a Cuban artist, who turned out to be Manuel. An artist of many talents, he is not only well-known for his paintings, but also for being one of Cuba's most prolific political cartoonists, having published his caricatures in the *Granma* (the daily state-run newspaper), *Juventud Rebelde* (Rebel Youth), and other state-run media for decades.

Manuel continues the work, now in the weekly publication *Girón* (named for the beach we know as the Bay of Pigs). Lampooning political figures in Cuba is no easy task, but Manuel has managed to walk the tight rope, having his fair share of works censored, only to be displayed like trophies on his office wall. Despite the delicate nature of his craft in a country without a free speech guarantee in its constitution, Manuel has garnered many international awards for his work (including a recent citation as one of the top political cartoonists in the world, not to mention having his work displayed in the U.N. lobby).

Sarita Murga and Manuel Hernández

On occasion I would see Manuel and his spouse Sarita slowly shuffling along Calle Medio, usually on their way to pay a visit to daughter Wanda and granddaughter Ingrid. After exchanging greetings Manuel always asked me about the *osos*, the bears. He was fascinated with the idea that Kim and I had a family of bears for neighbors, and how we competed with the bears to see who would get the apples from our apple trees. He even drew a caricature of Kim, ringing the bell she always carried with her in walks through the woods to advise the bears that a human was in their midst.

Even if I did not run into Manuel and Sarita in person, a day would not pass without my experiencing Manuel's influence along Calle Medio.

Several of his works were inlaid into the walls of the Kairos Center where we lived: a cross filled with images of country life, a peasant couple drinking water above the spigots of the purified water system. My favorite is a humorous set of restroom signs with the peasant man as Adam and the woman as Eve, to signal which is for men and which for women. Just down the street, one of his peasant couple paintings covers an entire wall of the coffee shop in Variedades, the city's large variety store. One of the café offerings on the menu is even called a *Manuel*, in his honor.

Manuel and Sarita are both salt-of-the-earth types, humble country people at their roots, with a quiet but biting humor. A story about his connections with one of the five heroes, Gerardo Hernández (no relation), reveals Manuel's quick wit. Before gaining worldwide notoriety as one of the Cuban Five, Gerardo was an aspiring political cartoonist, but his aspirations apparently exceeded his talents, leading to more rejections than publications. Soon after his prison release and homecoming, Gerardo received a commission to exhibit his works in a Havana gallery, and Fidel himself was present at the opening to honor the hero. Manuel was there as well, along with other cartoonists from the major papers. Gerardo made a snide remark about never having been recognized by his fellow artists, and how they were probably there at the opening just for the free food. Manuel retorted, *If we had only known you were part of the "apparatus" (government spy ring) we would have surely published your tacky cartoons.*

Across the bridge, I entered the neighborhood Pueblo Nuevo, i.e., New Town. Pueblo Nuevo is hardly new, with some of the more historic sites of the city located there, such as the first Protestant church founded in Cuba. The *Iglesia Episcopal Fieles a Jesús* (The Faithful to Jesus Episcopal Church) has indeed been faithful since its founding in the late nineteenth century. There is a built-in family ecumenical dynamic at work now, as Tulia, the priest, is sister-in-law to Orestes, pastor of the First Baptist Church. Also on the walk to the bus station I passed by a block housing some of the oldest of the African religion communities in Cuba, marked now by a large street mural illustrating the practices.

I reached the bus terminal around 5:30, the scheduled time for the bus to arrive, with passengers from all parts east. It had reached the station five minutes early, though, causing me to miss my opportunity to meet Sila disembarking from the bus, in hopes of repaying the warm welcome we always receive when the bus drops us off on the side of the carretera in La Vallita. She was cheerful nonetheless to see me, and met me with her signature smile, broad hug, and enthusiastic greetings of *¡Hermano mío! ¡Ay mi vida!*

We walked over to the taxi line, which is actually two lines, one for the state-run vehicles, which would either be an old 1970s Russian Lada or a Moskvich, either about as uninspired a bucket of bolts as you would ever want to see. Soviet design was far more utilitarian than artistic, leading to these square boxes on wheels, matching the square boxes of apartment buildings from the same designers. The other taxi line at the bus station is for the *máquinas*, the machines, which are the classic 1950s cars people have turned into private taxi services in the new Cuban economy that allows for *particulares*, their word for privately run enterprises.

Necessity being the mother of invention, a common generalization is that the fifty-six-year embargo has made engineers and auto-mechanics out of all Cubans, who manage to keep their machines running without the benefit of Advance Auto or Pep Boy stores. The classic taxis are more affordable, when you consider they will hold up to five or six passengers sharing the fare. As it was 5:30 in the morning and Sila had spent eight uncomfortable hours on a bus, I splurged and paid full fare ($5), instead of waiting for three or four others to join us, so I could get her to the seminary apartment for some much needed r & r before her conference began.

Sila had made the long trek to Matanzas to attend a two-day theological conference aimed at countering homophobia in the churches. On the short trip up to the seminary, she recounted a story she hoped to share in the conference. She had been to Camagüey, the capital city of her province, to visit her mother in the hospital. She had only enough money to hitch a ride one-way (on a cattle-truck converted into bus, costing only a few pesos), and after her visit she was waiting there in the area where a return ride might pass by, but she had no money to offer if one did. She began praying for God to send her an angel to help her get home. A man was sitting next to her, with dress and mannerisms very stereotypically gay. They exchanged pleasantries and shared a bit of their lives. A *máquina* stopped, and four people got into the '57 Chevy, waiting for one more to fill it. Sila's conversation partner went over and spoke to the Chevy driver, and then walked off. The driver motioned for Sila to get in, and she explained that she did not have any money. The driver said that her fare had been paid. Sila's prayer had been answered, and it mattered not to her that her angel had arrived as a stereotypically gay man.

I shared with her an experience I had in crossing the bridge into Pueblo Nuevo on my walk to the station. Focusing on the Lolo Gallery's flamboyant bird sculpture in the distance as I boarded the footpath of the bridge, I almost ran into an equally flamboyant scene in the foreground, a group of three or four of Matanzas' transvestite or transgender sex workers relaxing with a smoke, presumably comparing notes of the night's work. The *Plaza de la Vigía*, the tourist restaurant located next to the handmade bookshop, has become a magnetic area for a renewal of the oldest profession. Prostitution might have gone out with the Revolution, but it has come back into vogue with the economic crisis. I remember being with one church group eating dinner at the Plaza, and one of the travelers asking our driver and guide if the people hanging around on the sidewalk were prostitutes. The driver said all he needed to do was go sit at a table by himself and see how quickly he got propositioned.

I was happy to report to Sila that for whatever reason, I did not receive a proposition from this group of smokers as I crossed the bridge. We simply exchanged the typical greeting, my *¿cómo están?* followed by their *¿cómo anda?* I smiled as I shared the story, thinking of Wanda and imagining what her father would do with such a scene in his lampooning cartoon world.

Chapter Seven

6:00 A.M. – Bread

Now you know.
—Lennon/McCartney

To the Cuban people, America extends a hand of friendship.
—President Obama, December 17, 2014

Tu sabes.
(You know.)
—Cuban expression

Sila's bus was sparsely occupied on that misty April night trip, but the same could not be said for the buses making the east-to-west trek on December 17. They would have been loaded, max cap, with pilgrims headed to El Rincón, the leper colony located about twenty-five miles south of Havana. On the Catholic calendar of saints, this is the Feast Day of Saint Lazarus, the friend whom Jesus raised from the dead, who later became a leader of the early church before suffering torture and decapitation on December 17, AD 72. The Afro-Cuban religions syncretized this figure with the other biblical Lazarus, from Luke's gospel story of a certain beggar who lay at a rich man's gate, full of sores licked by the dogs, who desired to be fed with the crumbs that fell from the rich man's table.

Small statues of this figure, standing on crutches, skin covered in sores, accompanied by a Dalmatian, are a fixture in many Cuban homes. Some give the ubiquitous presence of San Lázaro credit for Cubans having such lovely, smooth skin, as he is patron saint of all who suffer skin maladies. The travelers making the annual pilgrimage to the Rincón disembark there in the Matanzas station for a few minutes of stretching their legs and getting a bite to eat before the last hour and a half stretch of highway. Vendors are there awaiting them, offering a piece of *pan suave* (soft bread) and a hot cup of *café con leche* (mostly milk, with a little espresso, plenty of sugar, and a dash of salt).

The bus station is not the only place to find 6 a.m. bread vendors. They are out and about the city, covering every block. They fan out from the Aguila bakery on the corner of Calle Medio and Santa Teresa, with their push carts or bicycle carts, and start trumpeting their wares. One U.S. visitor asked one day where the Muslim mosque was in Matanzas, having heard what sounded to him like the call to prayer repeated outside his bed and breakfast at the same time early each morning. The ritualistic call for bread does have the sound of a litany, and it does bring the Lord's Prayer to mind for me, at least a phrase of the prayer: *El pan nuestro de cada día, dánoslo hoy.* Give us this day our daily bread. Cubans do not stock up on bread. They, like the wilderness wanderers of old, have learned to go out and collect their manna each morning. There is something essentially spiritual about this practice, but I can't really say why.

I can say that there is something deeply satisfying about hearing that call from the bread man. There must be some kind of audition for the job of street vendor that requires deep, resounding bass tones of voice. *Pan suave, pan caliente* (soft bread, hot bread) became my wake-up call. Or near-wake up, as often I would stumble down to the street in a fog, trying to figure out the math of the coins I had in my hand, some in Cuban peso currency (*moneda nacional*) and some in the tourist convertible currency (CUC). The daily loaf was five pesos (moneda), and the exchange rate is roughly twenty-four pesos to the dollar, but on the street it gets rounded down to twenty, which means five U.S. cents equals one peso, all of which would be difficult enough for my poor math skills when I have a clear mind, much less when I am still sweeping out the cobwebs. On one occasion, a neighbor, María, saw the look on my face as I stared at the coins in my hand and she came over and picked out the twenty-five cent CUC coin and paid it for me.

If you are lucky enough to be walking by the Aguila, you can get any of the leftover loaves that did not get into the carts for three pesos apiece. That's fifteen cents for you math whiz folks, a ten-cent savings. In the Cuban economy, it is worth the effort to make the walk. On the morning of December 17, I was making my way to the Aguila, as the vendor was well out of shouting distance by the time I got down to the street. I loved walking by there, anyway, just for the smell. The old-timers like to wax nostalgic about the Aguila. Apparently in the pre-Revolution days, it had quite a reputation in Matanzas for its wide variety of bread offerings, croissants and garlic bread and cheese bread and the like. Now, it offers the one staple, the soft yeast loaf.

I was always aware of the danger of imposing too much U.S. culture into the Cuban daily life, but occasionally I got a dose of what my grandmother used to call the "cain't help its." That happened in the realm of bread. I never complained about the daily bread we enjoyed, but I did start feeling a hankering for biscuits. I started going to the "shopping" (a Cuban loanword that turned our verb into a noun to identify any tourist

CUC store) to scout out ingredients. It turned out to be a long search. Flour came in one variety, all-purpose, but it was several weeks before it showed up on the shelves. I bought a bag, and then came the search for leavening. None to be found. Anywhere.

I do not know where the Aguila bakers get their yeast, but it was not in any of the stores, not that I would have bought it. I was looking for baking powder and baking soda, which, in the right combination, with a pinch of salt, would make the biscuits rise. I finally gave up and sent an email to someone who was coming with a group from the States, asking if she could pack in some of these ingredients. The soda and powder arrived, and then came the search for shortening, which was never on the shelves, either. So I settled for butter, not a bad substitute.

**Stan making "pan d'eStan" in the seminary kitchen,
photo by Colleen Klassen**

Next came the challenge of a baking space, as very few homes have working ovens. They may have functioned at one time, but now most of them serve as kitchen storage spaces. The idea of stovetop biscuits was worth a Google, and sure enough, there were recipes. Lo and behold, they really do work. Three minutes on a side in a covered skillet over medium heat (fortunately, this was our hot plate's only temperature), and *voilá*, you have something that could pass for southern biscuits. I am happy to report that they were a hit. They became known as *Pan d' eStan,* Stan's bread. I served up plates of Pan d' eStan with all sorts of fillings: butter, honey and cinnamon, ham, cheese.

Few people went for my Slingblade-inspired mustard biscuits, but never mind. I still felt like I had made a solid contribution to the Cuban cuisine. However, given the challenges of finding the ingredients, I doubt these melt-in-your-mouth treats will be showing up on breakfast tables anytime soon. One of our seminary students, Rudiel, was especially taken with them, and tried his hand at Pan d' eStan, but given his need for more substitutes (cooking oil when there was no butter to be found), it turned out to be, as Cubans like to say about efforts that do not quite reach their goal, *Pan de Vecino d' eStan* (Stan's Neighbor's Bread).

Other fans of the Pan d' eStan were our friends Orquidea Lima and Lázaro Pomares, and their daughters Malu and Laura. We had hosted Orquidea in our home a couple of years prior, and so the fame of biscuits preceded my contribution to a meal in their home. Orquidea is the financial manager for the Kairos Center as well as treasurer for the Fraternity of Baptist Churches. While she knows her way around spreadsheets, her spouse Lázaro knows his way around sheet music. He is a professional percussionist who teaches at the local university, and plays in the municipal orchestra as well as in the ecumenical group Agua Viva, sponsored by the Kairos Center to preserve traditional Cuban rhythms and genres in church music. As confused as I get by numbers (math not being my strong suit), I get even more befuddled when trying to understand Cuban rhythms, despite considering myself a decent musician. Lázaro tried on more than one occasion to explain how the basic rhythm, the *son,* works, and just when I think I get it, my playing reverts to a standard 4-4 rock and roll beat and I remember just how *Yuma* (un-Cuban) I am.

I was delighted to run into Lázaro on the street that early morning of December 17, because I had wanted to wish him a happy saint's day and happy birthday (his parents had good reason to name him for the saint). He is actually one of very many Lázaros that I got to know in Cuba, all of whom I hoped to run into that day (there is the Lázaro of the church youth group, another from the Eastern city of Las Tunas preparing to enter seminary, the Episcopalian Lázaro from the lgbt group, and multitalented Lázaro who is at once a painter, sculptor, guitarist, composer, singer, prison chaplain, and contemplative prayer leader.) Lázaro the drummer explained to me that knowing all these namesakes was no accident. Many families, whether they are practitioners of Santería or not, like to hedge their bets and make use of all the possible resources of good fortune they can. Naming children after the beloved saint is one such way to seek some celestial favor from the cloud of witnesses.

Lázaro Pomares

Rhythmic Lázaro is another of those people I have trouble following in conversation. He is a rapid-fire talker, and assumes I am picking up everything he is saying. He has a way of following most sentences with the common Cuban expression, *tu sabes*, which always comes out as *tu sa'*, as the Cubans are as fond of eating the ends of their words as they are eating their bread. *Tu sa'*, i.e., *you know*, to which I always responded less than truthfully, *yo sé*, i.e., I know.

The truth is, when it comes to ordinary everyday conversations in Cuba, U.S. folks and other *yumas* can never know, entirely. Everything is coded, in what they call *doble sentido*. In a country without free speech rights, sentences tend to take on doble sentido, double meaning, with the second meaning generally involving something political (although they do have their fair share of sexual double entendres as well). I learned a bit about the political double messaging by watching the weekly satirical sitcom, *Vivir del Cuento*. Some of the meanings are not so hidden. The show's main character is lovable old geezer Pánfilo, whose name literally means *lover of bread*. One of the signature early episodes was about just this, the love of bread, as Pánfilo and his neighbor in the Havana apartment building, Chequera, cooked up a scheme to open up a bakery, a cooperative with their other neighbors. The comedy of errors that ensued illustrates the dozens of obstacles ordinary Cubans have in trying to make some "dough" in the new economy.

The gist of the weekly show is their constant struggle to make ends meet, to put food on the table. Another less than subtle message is in the artwork decorating Pánfilo's apartment: on his living room wall is a greatly enlarged and framed painting of the Cuban libreta, their food stamp booklet, to which he often places a small glass of rum as a votive offering. When it comes to the rest of the show's humor, I can only laugh at the slapstick acting, as I miss all the wit which comes in the form of one doble sentido joke after another. *Tu sabes. Yo sé.* (Not.) I have a goal of one day understanding Cuban Spanish in all its complexity–its rapidity, with the ends of words missing, and with double meanings. Then I could feel like a true companion to my Cuban friends, com-*pan*-ion. Sharing bread. When I shared that goal with a seminary colleague, he laughed and said I would only need three lifetimes to achieve it.

The actor playing Pánfilo is in real life a young man, in his thirties, who teaches acting at the School of the Arts. He was soundly criticized in an editorial of the *Granma* for making fun of the elderly and their struggles. The actor responded in a follow-up editorial, contending that he was not in any way making fun, but was giving voice to those struggles, and if it was in a way people could laugh at, well, that's the Cuban way. In a recent live show, the character Pánfilo joked about U.S. customs agents confiscating state-baked rolls he was bringing to his sister in Miami, testing them for traces of drugs and explosives. They found nothing suspicious, but could not believe the products were really bread. *How am I supposed to tell this guy that we actually eat this stuff?* Pánfilo asked. Even the best *pan suave* must get tiresome every day.

Bread became one of the bywords of protest in the late 1980s, when dissenter Marisela Verena recorded the song, *Son de Tres Décadas,* which became something of an anthem for Cuban exiles. *Salimos cientos de miles casi desnudos, desnudos de justicia y libertad, buscábamos refugio, pidiendo solo el lujo de ganarnos el pan con dignidad.* "We left by the hundreds of thousands, stripped of justice and liberty, we were seeking refuge, asking only for the luxury of earning our bread with dignity." Speaking of *pan*, Verena fled Cuba, like thousands of young children, in the early 1960s *Pedro Pan* movement, fostered by Catholic leaders in Miami who spread the rumor that the new Castro regime would soon be shipping the Cuban children off to Siberia for communist brainwashing.

This old-school style of dissent among exiles is showing signs of waning, though. There are those who are tired of singing the anthems, who are not willing to wait for a regime change to be part of the change in Cuba. Alberto González is one of those. Living in exile in Italy for sixteen years, he became a renowned chef, earning the prestigious Michelin Award among other decorations. He decided to return to Cuba after a visit to his dying grandmother, whose last wish was a bite of bread. He offered her a piece of Cuban bread, and when she put it in her mouth, her last words were *this isn't bread.* Her desire and disappointment inspired him to return and open up SalchiPizza, an upscale artisan bakery in Centro Habana, just blocks from where he was born. Why did he choose to return? "I think it's time. I believe that, if they let us, we are the ones best qualified to fix the mess we've got here. I want to contribute in some way." In another interview, he echoes Verena's dream: *No sólo se trata de tapar el hueco del hambre con pan, sino que éste tenga personalidad. Hay que comer un pan con dignidad.* "It is not enough to fill the hole of hunger. It has to have personality. You have to eat bread with dignity."

SalchiPizza's poppy seed loaf and the street vendor's pan suave are not the only bread options in Cuba, to be fair. The CUC stores that cater to tourists do occasionally have sliced sandwich bread on their shelves, a longer loaf than we would find here, available for a whopping 1.85 CUC (which converts to forty-four pesos, or two to three days' wages on average). For the Cuban economy, there are other bakeries bringing hard, crusty loaves out of their ovens. I am not sure, because I never bought any, but I had assumed it might be a little cheaper, due to its (in my opinion) lesser quality. I found out, though, that some people really do prefer it. There is a vendor in Pueblo Nuevo, an old man with a bent back, who shouts a different litany as he makes his way down San Juan Street: *Pan duro, pan frio* (hard, cold bread). I had thought he was joking, but I was told he had a steady clientele waiting for the hard loaves.

This is also what they serve up in La Vallita. Whether they have a choice and have access to warm soft rolls is something I never asked. The hard bread of the countryside matches the hard life experienced by the peasant people, but I hesitate to judge the relative quality of life in La Vallita versus Matanzas versus Fairview, NC. Without romanticizing or being nostalgic, I did get the sense while staying in La Vallita that this was the kind of daily life that produced the core values of my father and mother.

I recognize those values in the way Sila and Cheo and their family live. A hard life generates a strong spine, it seems. So I never complained in the morning when we were greeted at Sila's table with a plate of crusty bread. Often I would have the lyrics of a worship song running through my head, a song written by Lázaro Ceballo, the artist/musician/prison chaplain, who sings *unidos, unidas... compartiendo el mismo pan. United, sharing the same bread.* I discovered that this same hard bread at Sila's table was good for dipping into my café con leche. It was good for the dog, too, who enjoyed all the crumbs that made their way onto the floor. It made me think that the country people probably have a stronger connection to the Lazarus story, to the saint who dreamed of being fed with such crumbs.

Chapter Eight

7:00 A.M. – Coffee

Found my way downstairs and drank a cup.
–Lennon/McCartney

Today we are making these changes because it is the right thing to do.
–President Obama, December 17, 2014

después de café
(after coffee)
–Cuban justification for procrastination.

If the bread vendor's voice is the Cuban's wake-up call, the real reason to get up and wipe the sleep from one's eyes is the coffee. While Cuba may be more renowned for its Cohiba cigars, I would argue that coffee and sugar rank higher than tobacco for cultural significance, with sweet coffee being near universal as the drink of choice. Before my Cuba excursions, I was not a coffee drinker. I learned to like it several years ago during a month-long stay, when we took our meals at the home of Paco Rodés and Lila Gonzales. I had ample opportunity to acquire the taste, as all meals, along with various meriendas in between, came with the small cup of cafeicito on the side. Paco, founder and President of the Kairos Center where we lived, loved to quote the famous theme verse of the Protestant Reformation from the book of Romans in justifying his coffee addiction. While it is generally translated *los justos vivarán por fé* (the just shall live by faith), Paco preferred the lesser known Cuban translation (probably of his own making): *los justos vivarán por café* (the just shall live by coffee).

After acquiring the taste, I, too, became addicted. In our year in Matanzas, I discovered every door front family-run coffee shop within a mile in every direction from our apartment, and was a regular customer at several. I often wished Kim's dad, Ed Christman, could have been there with me, as he was the biggest coffee lover north of Cuba I have ever met, with the possible exception of my own dad. Ed loved repeating one of his lines from *Guys and Dolls*, when as Arvide Abernathy he stated that *coffee is so good, I can't understand why it's not a sin*. I started out "sinning" by imbibing the *Manuel* at Variedades, until locals told me I was getting ripped off with the five peso (twenty-five cent) price tag. They began showing me the *particulares*, where I could get the same cup o' joe for one peso (five cents), and besides, these family businesses also offered up the best chocolate bonbons and peanut butter fudge I have ever tasted, at ten cents apiece.

Girls outside a family coffee shop on Dos de Mayo Street in Matanzas

As I began writing this chapter in early November, the big news on social media was the viral rant about how Starbucks removed the snowflake from its holiday coffee cup, and is instead serving up its gingerbread latte and peppermint mocha in plain red containers. Somehow this is supposed to be the latest proof positive of a raging culture war against Christmas. I cannot imagine anything coming across as sillier to my Cuban friends, who would see the coffee-Christmas-commercial vortex as being utterly absurd on many levels. Which is not to say that coffee is not important to the folks in Matanzas and La Vallita and all parts in between. You could even argue that the tincture is treated with an affection tantamount to religious devotion, with whatever mug containing the sweet, hot, dark liquid being nigh to a holy grail. Some call it the nectar of the black gods.

To reinforce the idea of coffee's near deification in Cuba, several of our friends described the preparation of a good cup of espresso as a *liturgy*. Yivi, a petite young woman with a ravishing fashion-model face, is an artist and musician who became one of our adopted "daughters" (along with her partner Elaine, also stunningly gorgeous). Yivi makes her living as the Coordinator of Liturgy for the Kairos Center, and in that role she organizes many events and workshops around the development of rituals and litanies for worship and devotional life. She sees all of life as having liturgical significance, providing opportunities to be aware of God's gracious and creative presence. Liturgy is not confined to the walls of a church on Sunday morning.

Given that mindset, it is no surprise that Yivi, a creative artist with an eye for gracious beauty, views coffee making as one of the most powerful expressions of that daily grace. Indeed, she pours one of the finest cups of coffee in Cuba. Watching the expression on her face as she closes her eyes and lifts the cup up to her nose to smell the aroma is priceless.

Yivi Cruz Suárez

At the seminary, a close rival to Yivi for chief coffee connoisseur is Idael, a student from Bayamo in the eastern province of Granma, who is now co-pastor of Ebenezer Baptist in Havana. He also has an eye for sacred beauty in all of life, including the life of coffee making. Any time he was in the dorm kitchen with the cafetera on the stove, a crowd was sure to gather.

My mentors in the liturgy of coffee preparation were Orestes and Lázaro (the artist/musician). They take it seriously, it is a true *obra* (work), an *opera* in the making. Here are the basic steps. Pour cold water into the bottom of the cafetera until it is 3/4 full. Fill the basket with ground coffee, pressed down. Screw on the top of the cafetera, and open the lid. Place on stove on high heat. While waiting for the coffee to perk, put two or three teaspoons of sugar in a *tasita* (shot-sized coffee cup). Wait and pray. When the coffee first starts streaming into the top, take a dish towel to remove it from the stove eye. (Note: you have to have a dish towel handy in Cuban kitchens, because none of the cafeteras have handles anymore. In every home, there has been a time when someone put on the coffee and left the room, forgot about it, and the handle melted off.)

Using the dish towel, grab the pot by the lid and pour that first bit of coffee into the cup of sugar. Place the cafetera back on the stove. Take a spoon, and with the handle end, begin stirring the coffee and sugar together until it becomes a golden paste. While stirring, pray (remember, this is a liturgy!). By the time the paste is perfect consistency, the coffee will have filled the top of the cafetera. Fill the tasita with coffee, continue stirring, until the *espumita* (thick foam) has risen to the top. Pour this back into the cafetera, and if you have performed the liturgy correctly, the thick espumita will be on top, and will be in each of the three or four tasitas you can now serve yourself and your guests. As you sip the sweet nectar, your prayers are answered.

Lázaro Ceballo, photo by Kim Christman

There is a Cuban saying about this rite, for those who learn the art. *Ya aprendiste hacer café, ya te puedes casar.* It means, *Now that you have learned how to make coffee, you are ready to get married.* There was an embarrassing time in La Vallita, before my "liturgy" training, when I was told that I was not ready to get married (never mind that I have been married for almost thirty years!). Sila and Cheo had been telling us for a long time that we were family, but they continued treating us in some ways like guests. Namely, they did not want us to help out in the kitchen (probably for good reason). We insisted that if we were going to be called *Tío eStan* and *Tía Kim* by our "nieces" and "nephews," we needed to do our part. So they began letting us in the kitchen, to help chop vegetables, wash dishes, clean the rice. Finally, one morning, the family allowed me the privilege of making the coffee. I was nervous, especially about handling the hot cafetera with the thin kitchen towel. The coffee perked, though, and I served it up. Cheo was the first to start laughing. I had forgotten the sugar. Needless to say, it was a lesson well-learned, and a mistake that I never repeated.

If it is true that the just shall live by faith, it is also true that neither justice nor faith brought coffee to Cuba in the mid-eighteenth century, when French colonists fled Haiti during the slave revolts and introduced Arabica coffee production in the neighboring (and still slave-holding) island. Those French roasters found fertile soil and slaves to cultivate it in the eastern region, the Sierra Maestra Mountains, where 90 percent of Cuban coffee is grown. Just as there are different religious denominations with their own rituals, there are different liturgies to coffee preparation. In the East, the closer you get to these *cafetal* (coffee grove) regions, you find that they do it differently. I hope one day to make a pilgrimage to the Sierra Maestras and see a cafetal in person.

I have been close, with an eco-excursion in the province of Holguín to a family farm, where we got to witness how the beans are traditionally transformed into steaming brew. They are hand-roasted to a dark, strong, almost burnt taste, and then rhythmically pulverized and ground in a wooden mortar and pestle, called a *pilón*. Water is heated over a wood fire, the ground beans are strained through a cloth bag, and the dark liquid makes its way into the waiting cup with sugar to taste.

Idael, our Bayamese student, has family roots in the cafetal region, and he speaks with pride about how the peasants performed this work every morning in the countryside huts, and how they would find a common rhythm to the grinding. According to Idael, it was the percussive sound of those coffee beans being ground in the pilón that originally formed the basis of the *son* and other traditional Cuban rhythms.

Idael likes to take young people from the western cities on excursions to those eastern mountains. He finds it a great way to build friendships and community, to get closer to God, to disconnect from all technology and reconnect with nature. What is interesting is that this very type of project was part of the Revolution's education system until recent years. The *Escuela al Campo*, School in the Countryside, was one of the most controversial aspects of Cuban revolutionary society, with greatly divergent reviews of how it worked. Essentially, from the late 1960s through 2010, school children engaged in what we now would call service-learning or field education. Each year thousands of middle schoolers would spend forty-five days in places like the cafetales of the Sierra Maestras, harvesting coffee beans in September and October. It was a residential camp program. High schoolers would spend the entire year in the countryside, combining agricultural learning with traditional academic work.

This idea for the Cubans came from José Martí, who had written extensively about educational philosophy and pedagogy, and believed in the value of hands-on learning along with head knowledge. As far as this head knowledge, or traditional academic work, is concerned, the Cuban curriculum is filled with works of Martí. Unlike our country's multicultural educational system, which emerged from the "canon wars" of the 80s and 90s without any sort of common literary core, the equally multicultural Cubans decided early on to weave the works of Martí throughout the k-12 curriculum, creating a thread that binds their diverse social fabric together.

A favorite conversation starter of mine was to ask people if they had a favorite work of Martí. No matter the cultural context—rural or urban; east or west; black, brown or tan—people would have a ready answer, and would upon request be glad to recite their preferred poetry or prose. In Matanzas, Wanda and Orestes and Ingrid gave me a chorus of *Los Dos Príncipes* (The Two Princes). In La Vallita, Sila loves *La Muñequa Negra* (The Black Doll) for its subtle way of countering racism. Cheo had a hard time deciding his favorite, finally landing on *El Manifiesto de Monte Cristo* (The Monte Cristo Manifesto), which clearly articulated a call to the war for independence.

Lisy

Rut Vivian could dramatically recite all seven pages of the poem *Zapaticos de Rosa* (The Little Pink Shoes) while her little sister Lisy could do the same with some of the shorter *Versos Sencillos* (Simple Verses). I cannot help but believe that this "common core" is at least partially responsible for solidifying a set of values throughout the Cuban culture, as all of Martí's works–his poetry, his children's stories, his philosophical and political essays–all articulate ideals of community solidarity, fairness, equality and learning through experience.

In our country, one of the primary influences in my work in higher education, John Dewey, was a contemporary of Martí's and was advocating for the same types of experiential education. It is an ideal that I greatly resonate with, and spent a dozen years implementing programs of such experiential education in a college setting. I have to confess, though, that while it is an idea that sounds good on paper, whether a paper from José Martí or John Dewey, the experience is often less than ideal. To be fair, we always found our fair share of students who thrived in the field setting, found their passion, connected the learning, and they became our ambassadors, the stories we told to evaluators and funders. Another fair share of students always seemed to flounder, with some who would soundly and at times bitterly critique the experiences.

My experience can be multiplied many times over in Cuba. There is a fair share of Escuela al Campo alumni who give testimony to the great experience of those forty-five days in the coffee groves, the camaraderie formed, the team-building skills learned, the fun and games during break times, even the romances kindled. There are those who thrived in the agricultural setting, and found their passion. Cheo, Sila's spouse, loves farm work, and embodies the kind of deep wisdom and intelligence that it takes to run a cooperative sustainable agriculture project. Amaury, Sila's son, is another of those for whom the field work stuck. He thrives in his animal husbandry work.

On the other hand, there is a fair share of alumni giving testimony to the horrors of those forty-five days or the year in the countryside in the case of high schoolers. They talk about the violence, the bullying, the harassment, the strict military nature of the supervision. During Orestes' time, one fellow student from Matanzas was bullied incessantly, and nothing came from his complaints to the teachers or administrators. This student finally broke, and in the middle of the night took a machete and came close to murdering his tormenter who lay sleeping in his bunk.

It reminds me of the great gulf that often exists between good ideas on paper and good execution of those ideas. The unintended consequences of Cuba's experiment in experiential education exemplify some of the many ways Fidel has had to learn (the hard way) that winning a revolution is easier than governing. Sending middle schoolers to harvest coffee beans was supposed to be a way of forming the *hombre nuevo*, the *new man* of the Revolution. For the city-dwelling new man (and woman), the experience was supposed to lead them to appreciate and honor and respect the work of the campesino who grew their food. It had the opposite effect. Many of those *hombres nuevos,* especially the ones from urban centers who had been sent away from family and home at a vulnerable age, ended up hating the countryside, its work, the whole experience.

Instead of creating an appreciation for all types of work, the Escuela al Campo reinforced a prejudice and divide that has long existed in human societies across time and boundaries: the urban-rural division and the prejudice of city-dwellers against country people. I learned it early on, growing up in the suburb of Oakley that was populated by families only one generation removed from the farms. Along with my peers, I regularly made fun of the kids from Fairview (where we live now, on the old family farm), calling them *grits,* accusing their mamas of wearing *brogans* and betting they took driver's education on John Deere tractors.

In Cuba, Fidel was trying to undo a prejudice that got a new name in the War of Independence, when the country people got their nickname, *Guajiros.* This moniker materialized when the North Americans entered the war and saw peasant freedom fighters on horseback, poorly dressed, hardly looking like soldiers. The newly arrived saviors greeted them with derisive sarcasm, *Look at the war heroes!* The Cuban ears, unaccustomed to English, heard the words *war heroes* as *guajiros,* and did not catch the sarcasm, so they began calling themselves that. The word stuck. Sila even speaks of this prejudice that existed in the small pueblo where she was raised. It was not urban, but neither was it countryside. So when she began courting Cheo, who was from the country, and they announced plans to be married, people questioned her, *you mean you're going to marry a guajiro?*

Age-old and worldwide divisions aside, there is one thing uniting all Cubans, urban and rural, and again it has something to do with coffee. It is the universal distaste for and complaint about the quality of coffee they get in their monthly rations. For one thing, they do not get a lot, a small bag to last the month. Worse is what is in the bag: *café mezclado,* or *mezcla'o* in Cuban dialect, mixed coffee. The Sierra-grown beans are mixed with *chícharos,* aka chick peas, a filler that greatly affects the coffee's taste as well as its preparation.

I found this out the hard way, as someone gave us a bag of mezcla'o when the store shelves were bereft of Cubita and Serrano, the real thing. I engaged in the liturgy as usual, only to find the cafetera getting clogged, and very little liquid making its way to the top. After a lengthy wait, and a worry that the cafetera was likely to explode from the trapped steam, I gave up. Not knowing what went wrong, I tried again on another occasion, with the same results, and finally read the bag, which gives specific instructions on how to brew mixed coffee. One, use less water, and two, do not press down on the coffee in the manifold, and three, use a lower heat. The fourth instruction, unwritten, is add a little more sugar and hold your nose when drinking. Having a plebeian palate, I confess that I am not able to discern all that much difference (probably due to that extra sugar). Cubans are discerning, though, and have little patience for the faux café they find in the bodega.

The bags of Cubita and Serrano, when they do show up on "shopping" shelves, are way out of reach for most Cubans, given the ten to fifteen CUC price tag (a month's wages for many). They do find their way into homes, though. I suspect that besides being a popular black market item, this is also likely to be where some of those monthly remittances go, when exiles abroad send some help to their families back home. A bag of coffee or a pair of new shoes? No contest. It is a matter of priorities.

Despite having hosted around twenty Cubans in our home over the years, and despite having traveled to the island many times and having spent the year there, there is still not a lot I can be sure about when making proclamations about the Cuban people and their culture. Coffee, however, is a sure bet. There is not much they would rather do than sit down with a cup. When someone comes in from the kitchen with a tray of tasitas filled with the hot brew topped with foam, everything else can wait.

A couple of years ago, when Fraternity of Baptist leaders Orquidea Lima, Samuel Aguilera, and Marisol Muñiz were with us at a peace conference at Gonzaga University, I learned a litany to accompany the coffee liturgy. There were many activities that week, lots of presentations, workshops, meetings. As their host, I was to accompany them and make sure they knew what was going on at any given time. Every time I let them know of an upcoming event, I heard the same response, *después del café*. After coffee. They had found the campus coffee shop. Everything else could wait. *Después del café*. A good litany. A useful philosophy.

Living by faith, I can trust that someday we may resolve the big justice issues, the urban-rural conflicts, the capitalism-communism conflicts, the communitarian-individualism conflicts, the macho-queer conflicts. All in good time. *Después del café*.

Chapter Nine

8:00 A.M. – Street Life

A crowd of people stood and stared.
—Lennon/McCartney

Cubans have a saying about daily life: "No es fácil"–it's not easy. Today, the United States wants to be a partner in making the lives of ordinary Cubans a little bit easier, more free, more prosperous.
—President Obama, December 17, 2014

¿Cómo está la cosa?
(How are things? literally *How is the thing?*)
—Cuban expression

One of my standard routines after breakfast was to go and stand in the doorway of the Kairos Center or take a walk down to the river and people watch. The early morning fog would be lifting off the bay, and the river would be dotted with members of a rowing team putting in their daily practice. Calle Medio started coming to life at 8:00 in the morning, with the doors opening for the family-run cafés, the barbershop getting its first customers, the uniform-clad children scampering off to make it to the schoolyard assembly.

This last image is one that connects all Cuban communities, East and West, urban and rural, Matanzas and La Vallita: the state-issued school uniforms. Boys wear pants or Bermuda shorts (a cost-saving measure from some years back for the government to save on cloth), while girls wear suspender skirts or culottes. Both wear white shirts and kerchiefs that are color-coordinated with the Bermudas or skirts, with the colors dictated by the grade level. Primary grade students sport a bright red, middle schoolers a mustard yellow, and high schoolers dark blue for basic pre-university studies, purple for premed tracks, and brown for pre-tech tracks.

I had to chuckle several years ago when the pundits in our country were debating what could be done to stem the school violence. Some called for mandatory school uniforms to cut down on the gang identification attire. Others advocated for media censorship to cut down on the violent screen-time viewing. Still others wanted stricter gun control. They were all describing Cuban society, and sure enough, the formula works, if you want to prevent gang banging and school shootings, which are nonexistent in Cuba.

To add to the romanticization of this setup, I remember one of those early morning walks to school in La Vallita, when I accompanied red-clad Rut Vivian and her friends Karina and Natalie on their walk to school. They were my teachers that morning, pointing out and naming for me every type of flower in every yard (there is an astounding variety of tropical flora in Cuba), picking many of these blooms to form a beautiful bouquet, instructing me to take it back to Kim as an adornment for her breakfast table. There are no grass lawns in La Vallita, but the people are as proud of their dirt yards, regularly sweeping them and taking as many pains to beautify them, as any suburbanite in the states. These yards are brilliantly colored post cards in the making.

Back to the Matanzas morning: Along with the colorfully clad school children hurrying along the sidewalk, I saw Omar making his way from the farmer's market with his pushcart of vegetables toward his destination corner at Dos de Mayo. I saw the Stetson-topped Afro-Cuban on the corner dressed in all white like a Santería priest, heating up the oil in his churro cart (I became a regular customer for a paper cone filled with these deep fried donut-like pieces of sweetness), and I saw the young pop music aficionado Yosbel displaying his collection of pirated CDs for sale out of his front door. His day-long soundtrack for the street always included the widest mix of genres, from the long-running popular Cuban dance band Los Van Van to reggaetón, from Elton John to Motown. On hearing *Burn Rubber on Me*, I was delighted to share the small world story that a college acquaintance of mine broke into the music business singing background for the Gap Band.

On the morning of December 17, while *Somos Cubanos* was blaring from the sidewalk speaker, I noted a couple of women stretched out in front of the clothing store next to the CD shop. It looked to me like a scene of homelessness in our country. When I asked someone if this was a sign of the new Cuba (which presumably has not had homelessness for fifty-six years), I was told no, these were not bag ladies. They were early bird shoppers, having arrived in time to be first in line for the store's advertised dress sale.

Walking down Calle Medio, if you listen to the conversations on the sidewalk, you will hear an introductory question countless times, the same question that you hear repeated in conversations all across the country. ¿Cómo está la cosa? How is the thing? The *thing* in question is the daily struggle to make ends meet, to stretch the libreta and meager salary as far as you can in a month and seek out the remaining days' necessities in the black market. The standard answer to the question is the simple appraisal quoted by President Obama in his speech: *no es fácil.* It's not easy.

Working on *la cosa* is a full-time job for many, which explains a phenomenon that many first-time U.S. visitors find puzzling. Our cultural mythology tells us that socialism is doomed to failure because it does not provide people with an incentive for work. So the expectation is that in socialist countries you are bound to find lazy, unmotivated people sitting or lying around or engaging in phony make-work instead of putting shoulder to the plow or nose to the grindstone. You do not have to be in Cuba very long before you start seeing the opposite: hard-working, enterprising people, as busy and engaged as any capitalist worker-ant colony you would ever find. It is a conundrum. Without the highly touted profit motive to inspire a work ethic, they have nonetheless managed to become a highly educated and extremely inventive populace, perhaps motivated by pride, perhaps by a fear of impending hunger, perhaps by the intrinsic passion of the work or the benefits of a job well done. Who knows?

This is not to say that everyone walking the sidewalks of Calle Medio is headed toward some fulfilling occupation. There are always people sitting on the front steps of the church or walking somewhat aimlessly, with blank looks on their faces. Cuba has its share of unemployable folks, the mentally challenged, the emotionally disturbed and disabled.

There is the old man in tattered clothes, who would always come up to me and tell me in a somewhat rambling and confused speech that his lawyer had signed over the deed to his home to me, and if only I would come to his house he would give me the deed and I could take over residency. Then he would ask for a little help for filling a prescription. I learned later that giving him money would only go toward a bottle of rum, and it was no good giving him material necessities like soap (which he needed badly), because he would sell that to support his rum habit as well. The only sure bet in helping him was to take him to a local sandwich shop, order his food, and sit with him while he ate it, so that it, too, would not be sold on the street.

Another of the regulars on the street was Ana María, a thin, elderly black woman, also in tattered and dirty clothing. Occasionally she would have some paper cones of peanuts for sale. More often she would simply be walking along or sitting on a vacant doorstep along the sidewalk. Samuel Rodríguez, who retired this past year after many years as Coordinator of Social Services for the Kairos Center, shared with me an unforgettable encounter he had with Ana María. To be honest, it is unforgettable only because of Samuel's reaction to what for many would have been a forgettable request, something passed off as the crazy ranting of a street woman.

It was an ordinary afternoon, and Samuel was in the sanctuary for some reason, when he noticed her in the back of the church, sitting alone on the last pew. Though she was something of a fixture on the front steps, this was the first time he had ever seen her enter the building. There she was, hair disheveled, the same crazy look on her face, and her foul body odor reaching him before he reached her. He greeted her and asked if he could do anything to help or serve her. He thought maybe she was there for water or food. She simply said, *I need a letter from God.*

Samuel Rodríguez

Keeping a straight face, and treating her with the utmost respect, Samuel simply asked, not knowing what else to say, *Why is that?* She went biblical on him, reciting the Psalm that was on Jesus' mind in his dying moments: *Dogs have surrounded me. I am surrounded by a band of evil. They pierced my hands and my feet. I can count all my bones, while they look at me and make fun. They divide my garments among them and cast lots for my clothes. But God, you do not walk away, my strength, make haste to help!*

Samuel listened, and in response to her request for a letter from God, tried to buy some time, saying that he could not do anything at the moment except give her some food and drink, but if she would come back the next day, he would deliver her letter. He was curious to know, though, why she needed it, and what it should say.

As Samuel tells the story, Ana María, a "troubler of sleepy consciences," gave her answer. *The problem is that as I am black and my clothes are bad, they do not let me go into the stores. I want to go in, too, to see the beautiful things they say are in there, to get some fresh air, but they do not let me. They throw me out like I'm not a person. The people laugh and make fun of me. I need the letter so they will let me enter the stores and so they won't make fun of me. People are bad!* Samuel responded to this last declaration, halfway believing what he was saying: *But aren't there some good people?* The unfortunate woman shot back with quick eloquence: *Yes, but the good people do nothing.*

No es fácil. It's not easy, indeed, especially if you are mentally and/or psychologically challenged in this world, no matter where you live. Doors are closed and good people often do nothing to change the fortunes of these extremely vulnerable people who too often become invisible in our societies. *No es fácil.* Interestingly, though, there is a response to this oft-repeated truism that I only heard far to the east of places like Matanzas, in communities like La Vallita. *Pero tampoco es difícil.* It's not easy—*But neither is it difficult.*

People like Sila Reyna can make this claim, not only as a matter of faith, but as a directive, a mandate to do something about the challenges. In La Vallita, the difficulties of life are ameliorated by an open-door policy. The doors of Sila and Cheo's home are always open (except at night, as banditry, another of those occupations eradicated by the Revolution, has re-emerged out of the economic crisis, and their family, among others in the rural village, has been victimized by thieves in the night). Nevertheless, right up to bedtime the doors are wide open, welcoming the entrance of both neighbors and cooling breezes.

Many of the neighbors enter to use the telephone (a landline), as this is the only household with such technology in the neighborhood. Others simply come to sit and visit. Some are among the most vulnerable, much like Ana María in Matanzas. There is Rafaela, widowed, lacking attention from her children. She lives in a simple hut, dirt floors, no electricity. Her kitchen is a corner of the hut, with a makeshift fire pit on which she can heat her coffee or beans, with the smoke vented through the window. The church is helping her with roof repairs, as the rain has started leaking through to her bed. Rafa spends a good deal of time at Sila's, where she helps peel yucca, clean rice, or simply sit and enjoy the company.

Rafa is a pillar of the church, which tells you a lot about Sila and her church. It is not a big-steepled First church, complete with committee structures and performance choirs. It is a small group of twenty or twenty-five neighbors seeking open doors of community, many of them completely exposed to the cruel vicissitudes of life were it not for that community.

Rafaela is not the only vulnerable one occupying the pews of the little concrete block sanctuary erected in the backyard of Sila and Cheo's home. Other women who are similar to Rafaela in their struggle to survive without family support are there as well. It is all part of Sila's calling, to love, but more than that to show *preferential* love to the *least of these*. For her, loving them means making them feel at home. She has no ambitions for a big church with the status symbols of progress. She is in her element fulfilling the call to simply keep an open door and an open heart and to come to the aid of the hurting.

Rafaela and Nailen

Back in Matanzas, Ana María, without having any faith that there were any people who could come to her aid, still came to the church, believing that she could access a God who might intervene so that she could enjoy some of the simple pleasures of life afforded others. There she met Samuel, a fellow believer in God whose heart, I found, was every bit as open as Sila's. In telling his story, Samuel confesses that since he was not among those crazy folks who believe that God will do something crazy like write a letter to store owners, he assumed the responsibility of writing the letter. So when Ana María did show up again the following day, he handed her the letter from God. Here is what it said:

TO WHOM IT MAY CONCERN:

The bearer of this letter is My Beloved Daughter, in whom I am well pleased. I remind you that of such like her is my kingdom, as I told you a long time ago through another son, but you ignored him. Now I am sending her. It is a new opportunity.

Let her go into every store that she wants and treat her as if she were going to buy everything.

I also ask that when you see her walking aimlessly through the streets, greet her, smile at her, embrace her, kiss her, ask her, "How are you?" Offer her a piece of your bread and your fruit juice. Say to her, "When you feel hungry, come to my house and eat with us. Take these new and clean clothes and when they need washing, bring them to me."

When you do not see her in the streets, go to visit her in the psych ward. She will give you her smile of joy and infect you with that happiness which few have known, caused by your helping me to be true, believable, fair and good.

Remember that everything you do to her and for her, you do to me and for me and what you deny or do not do for her, or the damage you do her, you do to me.

Being sure of your careful and thoughtful and grateful attention in fulfilling my request, I remain yours forever,

God.

Sometime later Samuel saw Ana María in the streets, and greeted her. *Where have you been?* he asked. *I was in the psych ward.* After a pause, he remembered the earlier encounter. *And what happened with that letter?* He was not prepared for her answer. *I threw it away. They told me God was crazier than I am. Now they make more fun of me and make me feel more ashamed, because they are also mocking God.*

No es fácil. But both Samuel and Sila are among those working to make it less difficult. I wonder what they would think of the line in President Obama's speech about the U.S. wanting to make the lives of ordinary Cubans *a little bit easier, more free, more prosperous.* I doubt they would share the implication that connects freedom to prosperity. More often than not, it is prosperity which causes people to close their doors and gate their communities. It is something far more profound than prosperity that provokes people to keep their doors open, especially to those deemed crazy.

Chapter Ten

9:00 A.M. – Humor

I just had to laugh.
–Lennon/McCartney

The United States will come to dialogue with us when it has a black President and there is a Latin American Pope in the world.
–urban legend quote attributed to Fidel Castro, 1973

dar cuero
(to kid, to tease, to joke. Literally: *to give leather*)
–Cuban expression

My Granny used to say there were times when you had to laugh to keep from crying. In the never-ending *no es fácil* days when searching for the *cosa* would make many cry, Cubans have become masterful at the art of laughter. Ofelia Ortega, the famed Christian ethicist renowned as one of the founding mothers of feminism in Latin America, lent a theological lens through which to view this hearty laughter. She loved to speak, with a signature smile on her face, of the theology that Cuban church leaders developed during the dark days of the Special Period in the 1990s. It was called the Theology of the Absurd, with a basis in the foolish hope of the prophet Habakkuk who did his work in an equally desperate period in the history of Israel.

To push forward with good news of hope in the face of a hopeless situation, to laugh in the face of destruction, does indeed have an absurd feel to it, and the Cuban culture is the perfect place to tout such absurdity. For the Cubans are known for their ability to laugh at anything, to joke about everything. Ofelia connected the Cuban coping mechanism to the similar way indigenous women throughout Latin America find ways to generate joy in the face of tragic loss and oppression. The Cuban expression for this kind of kidding and teasing humor says something about humor in hard times–*dar cuero*–to give the leather.

I remember being at a Fraternity of Baptists pastors' conference in their retreat center in Guanabacoa. The schedule included one night on the town for a cultural excursion, some much anticipated fun and relaxation. As happens too often, the transportation fell through, and the disappointment was palpable. Before you knew it, though, Sila had the bright idea of forming a circle down in the meeting room, for some friendly competition among *cueristas* (leather givers).

I have never seen people laugh so heartily, as one after another of the pastors would stand and do his or her standup routine, with each punch line followed by a traditional song sung by the entire group. I wish that Orestes had been there. He has the reputation as being one of the quickest and wittiest *cueristos* around. He is never without a *chiste* (joke), a *broma* (practical joke), or a *burla* (biting satire). The thing is, I can generally understand him (he knows how to annunciate for *yumas*). On the night in question at Guanabacoa, I confess that I could understand precious little of the stories or jokes (these *cueristas* did not slow down for anybody), but it did have a familiar feel to it. It reminded me of the old Hee Haw show, when Buck and Roy would trade corny jokes, with a verse of *Cripple Creek* following each punch line.

Juanita Manrique on the piano, with Aracelis Hernández listening

December 17 was a Wednesday, and each Wednesday morning, without fail, gave me something to laugh at that I *could* understand: Juanita Manrique and her hilarious blend of music. Juanita, a dark black woman with gray hair in her early 90s, has an infectious grin and a mischievous laugh. For people who lived within earshot of the Kairos Center and First Baptist, if they slept late, they would likely *wake up to the sound of music*, a music designed to bring a smile on these midweek mornings. Juanita would show up at the church around 9:00, an hour or so before the weekly gathering of the *Tercer Edad,* the Third Age, their term for senior citizens. Instead of going into the sanctuary, with its stately grand piano, she always ambled over to the small studio piano in the salon adjacent to the sanctuary. Without introduction or fanfare or audience, she would start her concert.

The humor of Juanita's music, for me, was in her selection of material. She could seamlessly segue from flawless leitmotifs of one song to another, from greatly divergent genres. She might play a couple of minutes of a sonorous *Moonlight Sonata* and without pause move into the cannon-blasting section of the *1812 Overture* and again without pause sashay into a boogie woogie jam of *Roll Over Beethoven and Give Tchaikovsky the News.*

A time or two I hustled down with my guitar to play along, but I found that while I usually prefer playing if there is music around, with Juanita there was nothing better than sitting or standing by the piano and taking it in. Sometime between 9:00 and 10:00, members of the *Tercer Edad* would begin making their way into the salon. Pint-sized Nancy, retired custodian of the Kairos Center, would join in the fun, as would others, doing their best impersonation of ballet dancers as Juanita played Prokofiev, moving into the waltz for Swan Lake, and a rumba or guanguanco as she slid into an Afro-Cuban favorite.

On that morning of December 17, the diverse set list included some Beatles (*Yesterday*), a Bach invention, a Dr. John New Orleans stride piece followed by a bit of a Scott Joplin rag, then *We Shall Overcome,* and finally *Shall We Gather at the River.* If the sheer range of her musical memory was not enough, Juanita loved to mix up the styles. She might play the Baptist hymn as a Cuban salsa, and the Cuban *bolero* in the style of Mozart, and the classical piece as a blues. When she realized there were people around listening, she would simply look up at her makeshift audience and laugh, giving us permission to laugh along.

Juanita did not always stay for the *Tercer Edad* meetings, but occasionally she lingered long enough to enjoy the merienda. I loved to chat with her over a glass of mango juice and prompt her to share some of her fascinating life story. Her musician parents discovered early on that she was a child prodigy pianist, with the ability to imitate and play by ear anything she heard. They enrolled her in formal music training, so she would learn to read music, which she easily did. She read music unlike any of her peers, though. Once she understood the language, she could look at a piece of sheet music, and simply by looking at the notes on the page she would *hear* it in her mind, and would then *play* it by ear. Her university professors in the School of the Arts did not know what to do with her.

Stan singing with Sila and children of La Vallita, photo by Kim Christman

Sila Reyna, unlike Juanita, has neither musical talent nor training. She can enthusiastically lead the hymns and choruses on Sunday mornings, but the melodies are likely to drift from one key to another. Like Juanita, she understands the connections between songs and smiles, music and merriment. Whenever I had my guitar with me, she loved to coax me into playing some of the songs I had learned from Ry Cooder's Buena Vista Social Club project, traditional Cuban dance songs. I would break into *Cuarto de Tula* or *Son de la Loma,* and the kids would immediately start giggling. Sila would coax them up to dance in the living room floor, which would bring more laughter. We would wind up our impromptu set with a rousing sing-along of *Guantanamera* (the Cuban equivalent of "This Land is Your Land," based on verses of Martí). This song and its endless verses run through the head of every Cuban, drummed in from preschool on.

Juanita Manrique told me once that she always had music in her head, making it imperative for her to get to a piano periodically, to get the music out, or else it would drive her crazy. Some would say that explains a lot, because she has a reputation for a very peculiar brand of craziness. There is a French nun who appears to her periodically, in her bottle of milk (the Cuban government rations milk for the very young and the very old). The nun's name is Matilda, which is enough to make many Cubans laugh, as this is the name of an old brand of milk.

At any rate, Juanita occasionally shows up at the church and shares the latest insights from Matilda, who is very informative. The nun has convinced Juanita that there is an oil well underneath her home, and that once the well is discovered it will be the economic salvation of the country. I have not been to Juanita's home, but I have heard from others that she would greatly benefit from an economic upturn in the country, as her living situation is bleak. The unfortunate piece of Matilda's message is that she warned Juanita that one of the women of the *Tercer Edad* was attempting to dig a tunnel and get to the oil to capture it for private gain.

Another time, Matilda told Juanita that December 25 was the wrong date for Christmas. She said it could not have been at that time of year, because it was the middle of winter, and the shepherds would not have been out in their fields. It was later, in the spring. When Juanita asked why we had been celebrating it in December for so long, the nun explained that it was a mistake of the popes. So Juanita began writing letters to the bishop of Matanzas, saying he needed to begin a campaign to fire the pope for such a terrible mistake, encouraging him to get Christmas on the right day of the calendar.

Well, that was several popes ago. The absolute best of Matilda's messages had something to do with the new pontiff, Pope Francis. Juanita showed up at church one morning, not on her usual Wednesday. It was early December, and Orestes greeted her and asked if she needed anything. She needed to play the piano. Okay. But there was a reason why. She needed to be there to play the piano for the big national celebration. Orestes said that he was not aware of any celebration on the schedule. Juanita explained that Matilda had told her that there was going to be a big announcement: Raúl Castro was going to be on the news at noon, announcing that Cuba and the United States were re-establishing diplomatic relations. Not only that, but Matilda had informed her that this breakthrough was thanks to Pope Francis, who had been secretly facilitating negotiations between Raúl Castro and Barack Obama.

Orestes listened to all this and smiled as usual, thinking that Matilda was quite the cuerista. He told Juanita that she was welcome to wait until the news broke. She stayed, and played bits and pieces of Beatles and blues and boleros and baroque numbers. Disappointingly, the news never broke. That day. Just a little more than one week later, Matilda's prediction came true, down to the details. The milky nun was just a little off on the timing. If it were up to me, and if I had any influence over the Cuban powers that be, I would get them to send in some government geologists to do some drilling and check things out underneath Juanita's house.

Part Three

Heroes, Hardware, and Holes in the Road

10:00 A.M. - 3:00 P.M.

Chapter Eleven

10:00 A.M. – The Heroes' Homecoming

Nobody was really sure.
–Lennon/McCartney

*As Fidel Promised in June 2001, when he said: "They shall return!"
Gerardo, Ramón, and Antonio have arrived today to our homeland.*
–President Castro, December 17, 2014

¡No me digas! ¡Sí te digo!
(You don't say! Yes, I say!)
–Cuban exchange

As I began writing this chapter, I stopped to check on the Twitter account of one of the Cuban Five, René González. René had been released from prison in 2011 after completing his thirteen-year sentence, and after returning to Cuba began an ongoing campaign for the release of the others. At some point he started making use of the new tweeting technology for his campaign. Fernando González gained release in 2014, leaving the other three still behind bars. Today's tweet was a link to a lengthy blog by René's fellow hero Ramón Labañino, one of the three released on December 17. It is a fascinating saga, a memoir of the whole affair, from Ramón's being recruited into the covert project, how he and the others got into the U.S., what the operation was all about, and the pride he has in knowing that lives were saved when their intel thwarted terrorist attempts against Cuba. He also writes about the challenges of prison life, as well as details of the day of his release. This inside look at real-world espionage is an interesting juxtaposition to the *Spectre* of James Bond on the big screen this holiday season.

I do not tweet, but I do occasionally like to check out René's Twitter account, @rene4the5, given that it was from this account that Cubans first got wind of the prisoner release. At 9:59 a.m. that Wednesday morning, his straight-to-the-point, one-word hashtag gave the news: #VOLVIERON. Translated, *THEY RETURNED*. This simple message instantly activated the varied channels of Cuban communication, and through re-tweets, texts, phone calls, word of mouth, and for all I know homing pigeons (a big pastime in Cuba), the whole island was quickly aware that their heroes were headed home.

The Five Heroes (L to R: Gerardo, Fernando, Antonio, René, Ramón)
Photo by Hector Planes

Kim and I arrived at the Teatro Atenas in the Versalles neighborhood at 10:00 for a sound check and run-through for that evening's Ecumenical Community-Wide Advent Celebration, for which we were going to play some music. We were there on time, which meant we were about the only ones there (I never adjusted to Cuban time). Because we had our instruments to carry, and the theater was a couple of miles away, we had hitched a taxi ride from the Kairos Center to Versalles in Orlando's classic '55 Chevy. His car stereo played some classic nueva trova from the prolific folk troubadour Silvio Rodríguez, whom I consider to be something of a Cuban Bob Dylan.

Orlando with his '55 Chevy

With Silvio in the background (*déjame cantar fuera de tus fronteras, déjame cantar a los cuatro vientos*– let me sing outside of your borders, let me sing to the four winds), Kim, as always, engaged Orlando in some cooking talk. She had learned early on that a great conversation starter in Cuba was to ask people about their cooking. One of the first of these conversations had been in this same car with Orlando and his spouse, when Kim asked her how she prepared her mojito, (the topping, not the cocktail). This simple question provoked an elaborate set of instructions for the perfect formula in preparing the garlic, oil and bitter orange dressing. It was a passionate presentation (complete with constant q & a) that took us all the way from Matanzas to Havana.

That Wednesday morning, at the same time René González was tweeting and we were approaching the theater and comparing pork preparation notes with Orlando, Alan Gross, the freed U.S. citizen, was well out of Cuban airspace, celebrating the second day of Hanukkah with some kosher favorites he had not tasted in several years. Before the surprise holiday meal of corned beef on rye with mustard, latkes, apple sauce and sour cream, he enjoyed a big bowl of popcorn (which he had requested) with his travel companions, spouse Judy, Senators Patrick Leahy (D-Vermont) and Jeff Flake (R-Arizona), and Representatives Chris Van Hollen (D-Maryland) and Barbara Lee (D-California). Given how central pork is to the Cuban diet, and how rare it is to find beef (corned or otherwise), it is no wonder that Alan Gross had lost so much weight. It is definitely a challenge being Jewish and eating in Cuba, doubly challenging in Cuban prisons, no doubt.

We did not have time to get very deep into our culinary conversation before Orlando deposited us at the door of the Atenas. Kim and I carried our instruments into the largely empty auditorium, and were sitting there in the lobby waiting for others to arrive when Ingrid came running up to us, with great excitement showing through her broad, braces-covered smile. Ingrid is Wanda's teenage daughter, and her magnetic smile was not offered for just anyone or anything. While she was always polite (a word which her mother Wanda told me does not translate into Spanish), Ingrid always came across to me as the prototypical reserved teenage girl, unconcerned with the world of adults, no different from teenagers I know at home.

As a 50-something, I always feel fairly invisible around teenagers. Their world is not mine, and I doubt many of them share much interest in the things that interest me. I may be wrong. Ingrid strikes me as a mature teenager, smart, serious-minded, but like many teenage girls I know, she is introspective and spends much time in her own world, often the world of pop music. She regularly takes up residence in front of the desktop computer in Orestes' office, earbuds in, tuned in to a contemporary North American music video with lyrics (her way of learning English). Like some of our youth, she probably only knows Bob Dylan as Jakob's father. When not there, she is likely with her best friend Ana María (not the elderly street woman, but a schoolmate of the same name).

Evidence of the northamericanization of these youth is the lack of enthusiasm they have for the traditional Latino *quinceañera*, the highly touted fifteenth birthday debut event for the girls. Ingrid and her friends seemed bored with all the extravagant trappings of that tradition. She opted, instead, for getting tatted as a rite of passage. She spent significant time on the design, and even more time convincing her mother that getting a tattoo was a good idea. She succeeded, and now has a geometric design of her own making on the back of her neck. With their tats and cell phones and earbuds and hushed conversations, Ingrid and Ana María and their other friends could easily pass for a clique of North American girls, except they do not have to stress over the latest fashion fad (they get plenty of mileage out of their blue-and-white school uniforms).

As I said, Ingrid and her peer group were not easily excitable about anything adults would consider worthy of enthusiasm. So I was caught off guard when she ran up to me and Kim with dramatic news. I suspect we got the honor because we were the only people around, and she had to share the news with somebody. I am proud to say that we had a good conversation that morning as Ingrid filled us in, telling us that while she was not sure of the details (nobody was really sure), it sounded like Alan Gross had been released in a prisoner exchange and the heroes were coming home. I say I am proud, because we basically understood each other, which was a feat.

Ingrid Fundora Hernández, selfie photo

Until that morning, I had been constantly reminded in conversations at Ingrid's dinner table just how bad my Spanish was, how far I was from my goal of speaking Spanish with authentic Cuban accent and phrasing. We had many dinners together, Kim and I and Wanda and Orestes and Ingrid. I would launch into a story or a joke, and inevitably Ingrid would get a confused look on her face and look to Orestes with questions in her eyes. He would repeat what I had just said, to my ears saying it just like I said it, but once he said it, she would nod to acknowledge understanding. Orestes was my translator on many occasions, but he was not there that Wednesday morning, so Ingrid and I got to share the excitement of the news without the benefit of interpreters, and we were able to get the gist of what each other was saying, sprinkling plenty of *¡no me digas!* and *¡sí te digo!* interjections throughout.

I remember one of those hit-and-miss dinner table conversations being around the topic of the Five Heroes. An acquaintance of ours from the States, Max Hill, has been to Cuba many times, and on one of his trips he was sitting on the plane next to one of the high-ranking officials of the U.S. Interests Section in Havana. The two of them engaged in conversation, and the subject of the Five Heroes came up. The official laughed, and said the idea of them being heroes was all government propaganda. This official had devised an experiment that proved his point. He said he often stopped his car when he saw people hitchhiking, and would offer anyone a ride who could name all five of the heroes. He claimed that no one had yet been able to earn their ride.

I found the story a bit dubious, given the amount of coverage these five get throughout Cuban culture. So I did my own experiment, relaying this account at the table and asking Ingrid if she knew the names of the Five Heroes. Once Orestes translated the story and my question, she rolled her eyes a bit and rattled off the names, René, Fernando, Gerardo, Antonio, and Ramón. I asked if she thought all her friends could name them, and she said something like, *How could we not know them? It gets drummed into our heads every day at school and is on every test.* Maybe the Interests Section official only happened to stop for delinquents and dropouts.

I can attest that were he to be driving along the carretera and stop to pick someone up in La Vallita, he would have some quick passengers. They all would pass his test. The propaganda is not taken as propaganda there. Sila and family and church regularly prayed for the five, for all the families to be reunited. Some weeks after the answer to their prayer, we were in La Vallita, watching television on a Sunday afternoon. I was at the kitchen table, not paying much attention, when *Palmas y Cañas* came on. This live audience music and variety show is the longest-running program on Cuban television, having debuted in 1953. Resembling a mix of Hee Haw and Lawrence Welk, it is still going strong after more than six decades on the air.

On that Sunday afternoon, not too far into the show, Sila's granddaughters, Rut Vivian and Nailen, yelled out in sudden excitement. *The Heroes!* Sure enough, the storied five were there in the audience, making a guest appearance. Cheo came in to watch, as did Sila, and each time one of the faces appeared on camera, they all would point him out and shout the name in glee. The highlight was the end of the show, when all five were coaxed out to the dance floor to participate in the final number. There they were, five secret agent men, the spies who salsa, busting out their best moves to the delight of the audience, live and at home.

When I look at the U.S. counterpart to the Cuban Five, Alan Gross, and hear about the project he was wittingly or unwittingly involved in through the U.S. Agency for International Development (USAID), an organization that is supposed to oversee billions in humanitarian aid around the world but sometimes tries to act like the CIA, it leads me to surmise that our country's spies are a lot less 007 and a lot more Inspector Clouseau or Austin Powers.

The comedy of errors known as USAID intervention in Cuban affairs is downright embarrassing, to say the least. I had learned of the latest blunder only a week before the December release, when I was helping lead an ecumenical retreat for young pastors, sponsored by the Cuban Council of Churches. One of my sessions got interrupted, as we had a special visit by María de los Angeles, who is one of two directors in the Office of Religious Affairs for the Communist Party. She oversees the Protestant side of the Office, and is the person who gives the okay for the itineraries of all Protestant church groups and leaders who want to visit Cuban churches.

While it is true that the change of the Cuban Constitution in the 1990s brought religious liberty to Cuba, this liberty has its limits. Namely, the freedom to worship is enjoyed in exchange for a commitment by faith groups not to be involved in clandestine efforts to sabotage and subvert the Cuban government. The 1991 Central Report of the Communist Party, after acknowledging the importance of spirituality and religious freedom in Cuban society, adds this: *nevertheless, it seems necessary to continue eliminating every prejudice that impedes the uniting of all Cubans, believers and nonbelievers, in the virtue and defense of our Revolution.*

It is the Office of Religious Affairs that ensures the fulfillment of this commitment. For some, the tradeoff signifies a loss of the prophetic voice. For others, it requires learning how to be wise as serpents and innocent as doves, to know how to play the game and navigate the system in order to have a meaningful pastoral ministry to the most vulnerable–the sick, the hungry, the imprisoned. Still for others, there is no tradeoff at all, because they would not think of subverting the government in the first place. There is no conflict of interest for people who see the Revolution's values in line with Jesus' values.

Back at the retreat center, I came to a quick stopping point in my workshop, and sat to listen to María de los Angeles. While I had long heard of her, this was my first time to meet her. Some weeks later I would have the rare opportunity to go to her office in the Party headquarters to translate for a visiting church leader who got an audience with her. Here at the retreat, she launched into a tirade about the importance of young pastors being on guard against foreign interests who are insidiously trying to manipulate Cuban culture to subvert the Revolution. She gave examples of how USAID had long been trying to work through the monster's megachurches, churches who could bring wads of money and resources to the Cuban churches, but were imposing North American cultural values and a counterrevolutionary message along with their money.

Then María reported on the news that had just broken: someone had outed USAID operatives who had been working to infiltrate the Cuban hip-hop music scene. It was an outlandish scheme. The U.S. agents tried to cover their tracks by employing a Serbian music producer to court some of the young and notoriously rebellious artists like Los Aldeanos and Silvito El Libre. The Serb began trying to persuade these young artists to be more direct in their lyrical protests against the government, as the AP report said, *to pump up the volume of their protest songs* in hopes of fueling a "Cuban Spring" such as was happening in the Arab world (this was before all that began going south).

When the artists discovered they were being manipulated, they were outraged, on many levels. For one thing, for them to be labeled as agents of the evil empire to the North, as the Cuban officials could now brand them and their music, cost them dearly. Their music and hard-hitting lyrics suddenly lost credibility. Aldo Rodríguez, leader of Los Aldeanos, was embarrassed by the very notion that a Serbian stranger would be trying to mess with their lyrics to make the songs stronger and more politically charged, saying, *That Serbian man didn't even know how to speak Spanish. Who can believe that?*

The AP report breaking the story found the buffoonery of the plan unbelievable as well, saying that *the bizarre initiative was executed by amateurs.* Explaining how the initiative totally backfired, the report states, *Instead of sparking a democratic revolution, it compromised an authentic source of protest that had produced some of the hardest-hitting grassroots criticism since Fidel Castro took power in 1959.*

All this was not lost on María de los Angeles, as she spoke to the young pastors about the genuine frustrations youth are facing, and how these pastors need to play a constructive role in strengthening Cuban society for these youth, but to beware of these wolves in sheep's clothing who are willing to stoop to any level—to the hip-hop crowd or the church congregation—to try and subvert the Revolution and replace it with imperialist interests.

Her speech helped me understand some of the limits that were initially placed on our activities when we first arrived in Matanzas, several months prior. Our hosts, the Fraternity of Baptists, had proposed an itinerary for our year that included three sets of activities: teaching at the seminary, working with the Kairos Center in its retreats and workshops, and traveling across the island leading programs for the Fraternity churches in various provinces. María de los Angeles had approved the first two activities, but was not comfortable with our traveling on our own across the island.

I came to suspect, from speeches such as the one I heard that day, that she might have wanted us to be under fairly close supervision, not knowing us, not knowing whether we might be covert agents of USAID or some other lame-brained scheme to undermine support for the Revolution. By the time I met her, we were on good terms, and I was grateful that over time we had indeed been allowed to travel extensively to visit churches across the island. I trust that there had been some good references who had gone to bat for us, instilling confidence in the Office of Religious Affairs that we were okay.

I am certain that if we had needed a good reference, Sila would have come to our aid. On one of our visits there to La Vallita, we had a visit from the local official in charge of religious affairs for the region, and the conversation went quite well. We laughed when we remembered our first such conversation, a dozen years ago, when another pastor in another town told us to expect some people from the Party to come and interview us. The pastor warned us that these officials would be suspicious of us. They would not be as nice as the church folks, he said, *because they don't like Yankees*. Kim immediately shot back, *That's okay, we don't like the Yankees, either. We're Braves fans.* The pastor got a huge laugh out of that and made sure we related that story to the officials the next day, and as he had hoped, it broke the ice and we got along with no problems, glad to be leaving the spying to others.

The Yankee espionage scheme that employed Alan Gross was no more successful than the Serbian hip-hop plot. Secret Agent Gross was duped, he claims, into taking military-level technology into the country, without even being in on the secret. The technology he smuggled was supposed to be used to set up a Twitter-style account so the dissidents could easily communicate and disseminate their messages on social media. Every time any of these dissident social media efforts gets tied to USAID or CIA, though, and someone gets outed as having financial or technical backing from Goldfinger to the North, again, the whole thing backfires and the credibility of the critics is shot.

One of those hip-hop artists who lost credibility thanks to USAID was Silvito El Libre, (Little Silvio the Free), who interestingly enough is the son of beloved troubadour Silvio Rodríguez. While the famous father was continuing to lend his nueva trova voice in support of the Revolution, the son was voicing his hip hop version of a rebel yell. When the elder Silvio learned of the fiasco and the way Silvito and his fellow musicians had been manipulated, he had a yell of his own: *The USAID can go to hell!* That is probably as close to hip-hop as Silvio will ever get. His son's lyrics, on the other hand, are as raucous and offensive as those of his U.S. counterparts.

Which leads me to believe that when these three remaining heroes were released after fifteen years in a foreign prison, they were in for something of a culture shock that Wednesday morning when they landed back in Cuba. They came back home to a different world, with cell phones, tweets, and tatted teens who may only know Silvio Rodríguez as Silvito's dad, listening through earbuds to the rebel son's latest hip-hop rant. I can imagine Ramón, Gerardo, and Antonio hearing for the first time the sexually charged and vulgar lyrics of *Borracho Amoroso* (The Affectionate Drunk), and when they hear Silvito rap *no me digas mass que no soy un Santo* (don't tell me anymore that I'm no saint), I can imagine all three saying in reply, *sí te digo*.

Chapter Twelve

11:00 A.M. – Technical Difficulties

The lights had changed.
–Lennon/McCartney

The heroic Cuban people, in the wake of serious dangers, aggressions, adversities and sacrifices, have proven to be faithful and will continue to be faithful to our ideals of independence and social justice.
–President Castro, December 17, 2014

dale que dale
(again and again and again)
–Cuban expression

My first trip to Cuba came in the late 1990s, just about the time the five Cuban spies were being tried and sentenced. While there was a bit of light flickering at the end of the tunnel of the Special Period, the country had not yet fully emerged out of that shaft of economic despair. We saw that there were still shortages, and regular loss of electricity. I knew next to no Spanish on that first trip, and solicited Kim to teach me a bit. I asked her to translate a joke so that I could share it with the kids in Piedrecitas, where we were visiting. So some of my first words in Spanish were *¿Dónde estaba Moisés cuando se fue la luz?* (Where was Moses when the lights went out?) *¡En la oscuridad!* (In the dark!) Ha. The joke was a big hit, as I saw kids running up to parents repeating the question and answer with delight. My first contribution to Cuban culture.

I still love the joke. It's funny every time, but now it has a better punch line. We were helping to host some Cuban acquaintances just a couple of weeks ago, and when someone cut the lights out in the church I raised the question, *¿Dónde estaba Moisés cuando se fue la luz?* One of them answered immediately, *in the Special Period.*

The frustrations of the Special Period privation are still felt on occasion. Any dealings with light and sound checks for a big event could provide one of those occasions. I think about how many a.v. problems we regularly have at our church, and that's with easy access to the various stores selling equipment and cables and batteries and whatever else goes into making amplified sound happen. Amplify those frustrations one hundred-fold, and you have Cuba. The technology is dated and the supportive equipment and wiring are usually at least twenty-five years old, probably older. So I went into the sound check prepared for things not to run smoothly.

The scheduled 10:00 run-through really got started, as we might have expected, around 11:00. Before getting around to light and sound, though, every arrival brought more excited talk about the big news of the prisoner exchange. Some shared that television programs were getting constant interruptions with repeats of an important announcement: *El General de Ejército Raúl Castro Ruz, Presidente de los Consejos de Estado y de Ministros, se dirigirá a nuestro pueblo, y a la opinión pública internacional este miércoles 17 de diciembre en horas del mediodía, para realizar un importante anuncio acerca de las relaciones con los Estados Unidos.* "The Commander in Chief of the Army, Raúl Castro Ruz, President of the Councils of State and Ministries, will address our people and international public opinion this Wednesday, December 17, at the noon hour, to make an important announcement having to do with our relations with the United States."

Some people, like Luis Pérez Martinto, confessed to us later that the repeated message had gone in one ear and out the other, because they had heard "important announcements" of Presidential speeches so many times before. If anything, Luis feared it was going to be some kind of bad news. They had heard that enough times, too, to be attuned to it. This time, they *didn't notice that the lights had changed.*

If the lights of negotiations and diplomacy were changing that day, the literal realities of lighting in Cuba will take much longer to change. Cubans have a key phrase used often in dealing with the daily challenges of deferred maintenance and unreliable equipment: *dale que dale.* Loosely translated: *Here we go again. More of the same.* Our friend Duvier, who played drums in an underground heavy metal band in the 1990s, talks about the time one of the guitarists in his group had to climb a utility pole and cut a telephone cable to get wiring that could be used to string his guitar. Or the time he was at a rock festival and the stage gave way under the drummer, who kept on playing from the ground below. The show must go on.

Duvier is not the only one with stories to tell. As event coordinators brace themselves for getting it done, they love to recall past disasters. Every sound check and lighting check for stage shows or for church programs engenders story after story of equipment malfunctions. Like many stories, the breakdowns were anxiety producing at the time, but bring great laughs now. Our friend Harry from the Kairos Center was in charge of producing the Advent event, and as always, he had plenty of these stories to tell, such as the dancer with high heels who got a heel stuck in a crumbling stage floor.

**Duvier Quirós (right) with Sectarium,
photo from book "El Rock En Cuba" by Humberto Manduley**

My favorite is of the Christian hip hop artist who had a big following, and was rapping out a praise song at a festival, with the audience shouting back each line. As these artists like to do, he was practically eating the microphone, and when he made the mistake of letting his tongue touch it, a current of electricity glued his tongue to the mic. His next line became "Help me!" and the audience screamed back, "Help me!" He frantically screamed "I'm stuck!" and the audience repeated it back. He had to rap several of these call and response lines about his predicament before a stage hand finally came and helped unglue him from the charged mic.

Whenever I am at one of these productions, as people are getting all the amps and cables and lights set up, I cannot help but think about Sila and her community in La Vallita, and how far removed they are from these particular Special Period frustrations. Their family and the church are living embodiments of Gandhi's directive, *Live simply so others may simply live*. No frills.

It reminds me of when Sila came to visit us some years ago and spent a couple of weeks in our home. While we thought we were living simply, relatively speaking (no cable or satellite television, no dishwasher, no internet connection), it was a far cry from the simplicity of La Vallita. I laughed when she had the opportunity to call home and talk with Cheo and Anabel. To each she had the same line, the same evaluation of her hosts:

Stan and Kim are treating me wonderfully. They may have a lot of sophisticated things, but they are still okay. I did a quick audit of our "sophisticated things" that are lacking in La Vallita: running water and flushing toilets, washer and dryer, and then upon reflection I thought about the things that would not have been found in my home growing up, either: computers, food processor, central air, central vacuum, dehumidifier, air purifier, the list could go on and on. I was grateful that as far as Sila could tell, all that sophistication had not ruined us.

Back in Matanzas, Harry was leading the charge in getting decades-old sophisticated things to work for the big event that night, and telling the stories of times when things did not work as planned. Unfortunately for me, I have been involved in some of these fracasos, and before the rehearsal and sound-check could begin in earnest, I was coaxed to relate my embarrassing moments. As this December 17 event at the Teatro Atenas was my third such program in Matanzas, I confessed that I was a bit fearful of being a jinx, because of the breakdowns I had been involved in with the first two.

The first community-wide celebration had been at the Teatro Velasco, centrally located in Liberty Park, the town square. The room was filled with excitement, as this was the first time in fifty-four years that churches had been permitted to have religious services in the public square. I had not been at the light and sound check for that first Advent celebration, but I was on the program. I had been away at a prison chaplains' retreat on the eastern end of the island, and Wanda had called to ask me if I would accompany a singer on the program. Since it was a standard carol that I knew well, *¿Qué Niño es Este? (What Child is This)*, I agreed.

I got back just in time for a quick run-through with the singer, Yaima. I had to borrow a guitar from my friend Lázaro Ceballo, who was on stage playing with the group Agua Viva. All seemed set, and when our time on the program came, Lázaro handed me the guitar, I strapped it on, and walked out to center stage. The introduction and first two verses went fine, and then as Yaima started on the third verse, the guitar strap broke. I did a quick recovery, catching the guitar with my leg, and kept playing, while awkwardly trying to keep the guitar balanced. Fortunately, Yaima was standing in front of me and knew nothing of my awkward contortions. My friend Mark Siler was in the audience, though, and captured it all on his cell phone video camera. He said it looked to him like I had a sudden need to go the bathroom there at the beginning of verse three, and had to hold it until the song's end.

For whatever reason, this near-disaster did not dissuade Wanda from recruiting me to play again the following year. This time the event was to be outside, in the Liberty Park, which generated even more excitement, as no religious event had been held there for fifty-five years or more. For this event, Wanda gave me an old Cuban Christmas carol to learn, and I was to accompany a singer named Mayuley. It was a complicated song, for me, with a traditional Cuban rhythm and a minor key verse that morphed into a major key chorus. I did my due diligence of wood-shedding, until I felt I had it down pat, and with a week or so to go before the event I was ready to try it out with Mayuley.

Before I met her, I began to get the idea that I was in over my head. Several times people had asked me if I was planning to attend the Advent celebration, and each time I responded that I was on the program, that I was going to accompany Mayuley, and each time I got a response of open-mouthed wonder, *Mayuley? Wow.* I discovered they were not exaggerating with their wonder. I learned that she was one of Cuba's finest voices, a world traveling artist who had won many prestigious awards and was coming to town from nearby Varadero Beach, where she had a standing gig at one of the resort hotels whenever she was in between stops on her international tour.

I was stunned when Mayuley walked into the church that afternoon for the run-through. Here was this incredibly glamorous woman, long thick hair and gorgeous smile, elegantly dressed. She was not familiar with the song we were to do, but was able to sight read music with no problem, so away we went, executing the difficult piece without a single snag. Her voice was to die for. While I could not really say why we needed to, I asked if we could run through it a second time, just to be sure. Same thing, picture perfect.

What with the random responses I had been getting to the prospects of accompanying Mayuley, and what with the sound of that golden voice still in my head, when the event day came around I went in the afternoon for the sound check with my head a few sizes too big. While I was comfortable with the song, I did not have it memorized, so I took the sheet music and a music stand over to the park. Our good friend Pancho from the Mirón Theater was in charge of logistics for this event. He and his crew were engaged in the usual searching for cables to replace those that did not work, and it took a while to find an extension cord to plug in my guitar effects pedal, but finally there was sound, and I was feeling good. Too good.

As the sun set and the hour of the performance approached, I went back up on stage to make sure everything was in order, and discovered that the only lights were in front of me, so the music on the music stand was dark. My first frantic moment. I hustled to find some paper, quickly wrote down the minor chord sequence of the verse and major chord sequence of the chorus, found some scotch tape, and attached it to the edge of my guitar. If I leaned a bit forward, I could get this scrap of paper in the light and read the makeshift chart. Okay, one problem solved, just like the Cubans might have done.

Then, five minutes before the beginning of the program, Wanda ran up to me with a young woman who was to sing in the program, and the anxious looks on their faces told me more ingenuity was in order. She had her background music on a flash drive, but her drive would not play through Pancho's computer. They asked if I could accompany her. What song? Predictably, it was not a song I knew. Wanda said not to worry, the woman could sing it to me and I could learn it. The sweat started pouring at that prospect, but I did not want to disappoint Wanda, and so there I was, behind the stage with a woman singing in my ear and me trying to find chords to go along. Unlike Mayuley's song, this one was blessedly simple, contemporary with a straight-ahead North American rhythm, and we got close enough for jazz, as they say. The show must go on, and it did, with a park filled with people already getting emotional and weeping, even before the first song.

On the other side of the park several teenagers from the church were in costume and face paint, motionless in a mime-statue version of the holy family with angels. They stayed that way throughout the entire program, with people walking by to gaze in wonder throughout the night. My newly learned song was third or fourth in the program, and while the first few groups did their numbers, I had fingers in my ears, humming the tune so as not to forget it. When it was our turn, I took a deep breath and played like it was an old favorite, trying not to let my anxiety and sweat show as she sang, and I breathed a heavy sigh of relief as we finished the number with no apparent problems.

After a few more performances from a duet and string quartet and brass ensemble, it was our turn. Mayuley, decked out in a killer red dress, climbed the stairs to the stage, and I followed. I got the guitar strapped on and leaned forward to see the illuminated scrap of paper taped on its edge, took another deep breath, and started the intro.

I looked over and noticed that Mayuley was trying to arrange her piece of sheet music on the music stand. I had not thought about her being in the same predicament as me, and I secretly hoped that her much younger eyes were better than mine and she would be able to see in the dim light. At first I thought my wish was granted, as she sang the verse flawlessly, but then the unexpected happened. While we both modulated for the chorus, she modulated into a different major key than me. *Ay caramba*–two run-throughs of an unfamiliar song were not enough!

Immediately my mind was racing. *What should I do? Stop and start over? Try to figure out what key she's singing in? Or just play through it, in two different keys?* I opted for the latter, trying not to show any distress on my face, even as the nervous sweat intensified. At the end of the chorus, the song changes back into the minor key for verse two, and thankfully, we were back in the same key. Just like in the first chorus, though, we again went our separate ways. We were back together for verse three. All through that verse, I was dreading the oncoming chorus, knowing there was little chance we would get it right. My fears were well-founded, as the third chorus again sounded like a discordant John Gage arrangement, with singer in one key and accompanist in another for some kind of avant-garde experiment.

Mayuley Alvarez with Stan at 2014 Advent Celebration in Liberty Park, photo by Orestes Roca

The show went on, and concluded with people weeping for joy as all the groups united on stage to lead the audience in *Silent Night*. Mayuley and I had an awkward hug, with me trying to apologize for not leading her well enough, and then I discovered a curious thing. While this is no scientific survey, I suspect that around 80 percent of people do not have a great musical ear. Because as I got my stuff together to take back to the church, that is roughly the percentage of people who came up to me to say that our song was the most beautiful thing they had ever heard. The other 20 percent who knew what had happened just shook their heads and smiled, acknowledging that I had been in a tight spot. They enjoyed pointing at the cameras around, reminding me that this event would be nationally televised.

I would never have to worry about such a musical faux pas in La Vallita. While the congregation sings heartily, with great fervor, there are always several who are singing in different keys. In addition, there are no issues with lights. Well, that is not exactly true, but the issues are far different from the challenges in Liberty Park or the Velasco Theater. A few years ago, Sila and the church moved from meeting in the living room to a bona fide sanctuary. They constructed a simple block structure in the back yard, with the ceiling little more than six feet high, and an extension cord providing current for the one light illuminating the space. No speakers, no mics, no frills.

Their one frustration around lights happened in December, during the Advent season, when Sila added four more lights–the candles of a simple Advent wreath–to the sanctuary. She immediately had to fend off the criticism of a new member who had moved to the community, who had been part of a fundamentalist church. He claimed that the wreath was of the devil, and had no place in a true house of worship. Sila explained the tradition of the wreath, and what the candles signified, but this man's anti-Catholicism was so ingrained that any religious candle-lighting smacked of Popish influence. Sila's refusal to bow to his demands led him to leave the church for purer pastures with the Pentecostals.

While this kind of conflict gets repeated a lot, it does not seem to faze her a bit. She and the church stay true to their course of living simply and loving simply so that others can simply live and love. They embody as much as anyone President Castro's words of resilience: *The heroic Cuban people, in the wake of serious dangers, aggressions, adversities and sacrifices, have proven to be faithful and will continue to be faithful.*

Dale que dale.

Chapter Thirteen

12:00 noon – Lunch

They'd seen his face before.
–Lennon/McCartney

While acknowledging our profound differences, particularly on issues related to national sovereignty, democracy, human rights and foreign policy, I reaffirm our willingness to dialogue on all these issues.
–President Castro, December 17, 2014

¿Qué bolá, acere?
(What's happening, homeboy?)
–Afro-Cuban street greeting

After all the storytelling subsided, the sound and light rehearsal came off with no apparent glitches, smooth sailing. Performers and crew celebrated with a merienda brought in by Julio César, who serves as something of the quartermaster for the Kairos Center. Knowing where to find the best deals on everything, on this morning a smiling Julio came in with a box full of hot dogs, a rare treat. Between bites of the tasty snack we raised a cup of the slushy pineapple juice in a toast to the successful morning. The only equipment challenge had been finding a table for Kim's tabletop hammer dulcimer. Nothing resembling a small table was to be found in the theater. We made do with a chair, and were good to go.

Julio accompanied us part way to the seminary, where we were going to eat lunch with our students. Along with being the resident expert on which state-run *bodega* or privately owned *particular* to buy anything and everything on the Cuban budget, he also knows every street and shortcut in Matanzas. He makes rounds through the various neighborhoods every Friday, as the deliverer of the Kairos Center's version of a meals-on-wheels program. The wheels in Julio's case is his bicycle, with the meals stacked in a makeshift box attached to the bike.

Julio César Valdes Ruiz, photo by Nancy Bradley

With medium height and slight build and short black hair starting to show some premature gray, Julio César does not draw as much attention as he did a few short years ago, when he sported long curly hair that hinted at his affection for rock and roll. His love for the Beatles is only topped by his fanaticism over the world of heavy metal, the heavier the better. Without Julio's tutelage, I would never have known about the underground metal club scene in the history of Cuban music, places where young people thrashed each other in mosh pits to the music of bands like Sepultura, a Brazilian group hugely popular outside the U.S. who helped generate the death metal and thrash metal genres in the 1980s and 90s. This is not your father's Buena Vista Social Club.

Julio was sent to accompany us so we could get to lunch on time (the bell rings at 12:30 for the seminary lunch crowd). *Hasta la comida siempre (to the meal, always)* had become my standard pre-meal joke, a takeoff on Che's famous revolutionary slogan *hasta la victoria siempre (onward the victory, always)*, written at the close of his goodbye letter to Fidel. Backtracking the way we knew, the long way around, would have taken us forty-five minutes to get to the meal. A shorter route would take us through the Marina neighborhood, historically known as the "bad" barrio of Matanzas, caused by the port's presence of sailors, which historically meant the accompanying presence of alcohol and prostitution.

The Marina also has the greatest concentration of Afro-Cuban religious practitioners in Matanzas, and the prejudices of *Gallegos* (the lighter-skinned Spanish descendants), both racial and religious, still linger, creating fears of white folks like us walking through the Marina unaccompanied. To be sure, I did walk through the neighborhood alone on many occasions, usually searching for one grocery item or another that was missing from shelves in the stores I was prone to frequent, and I never once felt the least bit frightened or intimidated. Perhaps part of that is because of the twenty-year work the Kairos Center has done and continues doing in the Marina, forming relationships and alliances, supporting community organizing and self-empowerment projects. They had seen light-skinned faces before. Even so, Julio came along, exchanging *qué bolá's* with people he passed. I was glad for his presence, not as protector, but as guide through the twists and turns that would get us to the seminary.

There were not that many *aceres* on the streets that day. Some had gone on the San Lázaro pilgrimage to the leper colony. Others were inside, glued to their TV, listening to Raul's historic speech announcing the prisoner release and the new day in Cuban-U.S. relations. When *El Chino* (the Cubans' nickname for their president, probably not voiced too loudly in public) spoke of the profound differences on issues related to things such as democracy and human rights, he was of course referring to the differences between our two countries. He could just as easily have been referencing the profound differences that have arisen within the Cuban populace around these very issues.

I think of the depth of traditional revolutionary belief Sila Reyna has in fundamental human rights, such as the right of all people to have something to eat. As we were walking *hasta la comida*, I remembered the time our pastor Steven and his family traveled with us to La Vallita to meet Sila and her family and church. As the midday mealtime approached, the house filled with more mouths to feed, including Karina, Rut Vivian's best friend, who was always there at mealtime. Sila explained to Michelle, Steven's spouse, that they had learned some time back that Karina's mother was finding it difficult to meet the challenge of stretching her food dollar. Sila's next words greatly affected Michelle: *Our family knows that if someone in the community isn't eating, we can't eat.* So like the widow from Zarepheth in the Elijah story, they were always willing to share whatever they had, even if it was their last meal.

In Sila's mind, while socialism is not perfect, it is as close to the gospel as anything she has seen or heard of that humans have come up with, and she says that the great work of the church, and of Cuban society, is to be about the business of perfecting socialism, until the utopian dreams of a beloved gospel community are fulfilled. What struck Steven as remarkable was one of the initial conversations he had with this pastoral colleague. Here she sat, in a relatively impoverished community, in a home with no running water, and she was enthusiastically talking about her thesis research, on how to appropriate Jürgen Moltmann's theology of hope in the context of her community and its daily challenges. Steven had not expected a lesson on German theology and utopian philosophy in the boondocks of an underdeveloped country. That did not compute with his prior experiences of "mission trips" where we developed folks bring our wisdom and resources to the poor.

Julio César led us on the serpentine route through the Marina, and when we got to a familiar street closer to the center of town, we parted ways. He turned back to be about his work, and we climbed the hill to the seminary. We got there a bit after the sounding of the bell, and entered as the students and faculty and staff were singing the grace: *demos gracias al Señor, demos gracias, por los alimentos hoy....* (we give thanks to the Lord. We give thanks for today's food).

It was a good while before we ever learned the clever *doble sentido* way that some of the more dissident minded singers accentuated the words of this blessing, smiling mischievously as they turned it into a different kind of prayer: a plea for *democracia* (democracy) in place of *demos gracias,* the routine thanksgiving for the food. Since the Cubans generally eat that final *s* in the words, the replacement sounded close to a homonym.

Walchidea, Mamita, and Kim in seminary kitchen

Before finding a table with a couple of empty spots, we went over to the window separating the kitchen from the dining room, to greet Mamita and Walchidea, the jovial cooks and bottle washers. As Mamita decided early on not to try to pronounce my name, I always enjoyed hearing her greet me as *profe*. She had seen me bring the guitar into the cafeteria, and asked if I was going to play some Beatles.

It was a delight when we discovered she was a Beatles fan, and she had been thrilled to have been serenaded on her birthday with her favorite: *Let It Be*. I told her no, that I had brought it for a rehearsal of the wedding we were to play at the next day. No sooner had I said "no" than the Dekano–the Dean–another fan of the Fab Four, approached me to ask if I would play at the banquet that evening. *Sure*, I said, *what song did you have in mind? Pues*, he responded, *given the news of the day, I think it would be appropriate for us all to sing "Imagine."*

We found our seat with some of the Baptist students, and began passing the various platters around. Rice, beans, aselga (greens from the seminary garden). *What's the meat of the day?* The familiar platter of croquets always provoked that question, so someone could respond with the punch line of the joke that never seemed to get old: *Ave*. Another clever play on words. *Ave* means *bird*, but in this context, it is shorthand for *averiguar– find out*, i.e., *who knows?* Mystery meat exists across our borders. I often found myself longing for a couple of packets of Heinz ketchup.

At the table next to ours, a heated debate was already underway, in response to the news of the day. Faculty, staff, and administrators were trying to *averiguar*–to find out–what the implications were of this new day in diplomacy. There was no argument about the merits of the decision itself. Unlike many Miami Cubans, everyone I knew agreed that renewed diplomacy and relations were fifty years overdue. Even among dissenters, there was a common-sense understanding that the blockade had not served any good function, other than to give the government a convenient whipping boy on which to blame every failure. The argument raged instead over what was likely to follow in the wake of the news. Who would benefit? Whose interests would be served? What would the government do once there was no scapegoat on which to place all of its sins?

The views ranged from cheery optimism to guarded cynicism. Signals were already evident that the regime was placing all of its economic hopes on the tourism sector, and that was likely to impact only a very thin slice of the population. Other signals gave rise to fears that the new relations were paving a one-way street of economic trade, with North American goods showing up in greater abundance in the CUC stores, while the blockade would remain on fifths of Havana Club showing up in our ABC stores or Cohibas showing up in our cigar stores. Still, even with skepticism and cynicism, there was genuine excitement and enthusiasm that there was even something to talk about, after fifty-six years of frozen hopes.

The enthusiasm that started with the spread of René González' social media post had grown throughout the morning as people had gotten word of his continued updates on Twitter. After his initial *VOLVERAN*, he tweeted the news as he got it of the accelerated release date for each of his fellow heroes. First came Gerardo's news: *The Office of Federal Prisons changed the date of Gerardo's exit to today.* Then a bit later: *With Ramón the same has happened: they changed the exit date to today.* Later in the morning came this: *And at last Tony, he also has a date change for today.*

We would have one of those two degrees of separation experiences with this last hero, as our friend Tony, a pastor in Matanzas who is vice-president of the Council of Churches, met the newly freed Tony at an event sponsored by the Council to celebrate the answer to prayer. At this event the spy Tony expressed gratitude for those long years of support and prayer from the Cuban churches, and while he is not a person of faith, he did express gratitude for the Bible, as it was the only reading material in his cell for years, and it kept his mind engaged. He had been surprised by its message of hope and liberation, and he appreciated that. When Pastor Tony told us this story, I could not help but think about Karl from Slingblade, who had also read the Bible through while serving time, saying *I reckon I understand a great deal of it. It wasn't what I expected.*

As I sat and listened to our students and to the adjoining table's dialogue and debate, my mind wandered to what kind of conversations were happening in La Vallita. I suspected that Sila was voicing thanksgiving for the answer to years of fervent prayer for the heroes to all be back on their home soil. In her home, the accent would always be clear on *demos gracias* (she loved singing all five verses to the mealtime song). Not that she was unfamiliar with *democracia*. I thought about the visit she had made to our democratic soil, only a year and a half earlier. I am sure everything was not as she had expected. For one thing, she celebrated the liberty embedded in our society that allowed her to freely enter elementary and high schools and talk to students about life in Cuba with no vetting or oversight. She said this would not happen in Cuba with U.S. visitors.

On the other hand, Sila observed the extremes of life demonstrated by a democracy where the ideal focuses on individual achievement and accomplishment instead of community and the common good. We took her to the Biltmore House, touted as "America's Finest Castle," to see an extreme of conspicuous consumption. Later we took her to the Haywood Street Church, a congregation largely composed of homeless people just up the road from the Biltmore. Poverty and hunger in the shadow of extreme wealth. Along the route from Biltmore to Haywood, she noted all the billboard advertisements, promoting materialism instead of ideals of justice as they do in Cuba (one of the reasons the faces of the five were so familiar was the proliferation of billboards promoting their cause).

There is no doubt that Sila, with her pastoral heart and her ethic of hopeful love, felt more at home on Haywood Street than at the Biltmore House. She felt some sense of solidarity with the masses. She talked about the emphasis they have in Cuba on the *masas*, the *masses*, a word that in the singular means *dough*, and is used to speak of the unity of the Cuban people, in contrast to the individual kernels of grain emphasized in an individualistic society. One of the common billboards seen along the Cuban highway has a quote of Fidel: *El genio está en las masas, el genio es masivo*. The genius is in the masses. The genius is massive.

While the *masa* is losing its form in Cuba, especially in Havana with newly emerging class divisions, places like La Vallita still experience life in solidarity. The western cities have their hopes, to be sure, based on anticipated access to more Nike and Apple products. But Sila's hopes are different, based not only on her utopian ideals of perfecting socialism, but on the theology of people like Jürgen Moltmann, with whom she resonates when he writes: *Whenever we base our hope on trust in the divine mystery, we feel deep down in our hearts: there is someone who is waiting for you, who is hoping for you, who believes in you.* Sila would have been voicing gratitude for the family and community of support that had been waiting and hoping and believing for fifteen years that there would be a day to welcome Tony and Ramón and Gerardo back to their homes.

Chapter Fourteen

1:00 P.M. – Deferred Maintenance

And though the holes were rather small...
—Lennon/McCartney

This in no way means that the heart of the matter has been solved. The economic, commercial, and financial blockade, which causes enormous human and economic damages to our country, must cease.
—President Castro, December 17, 2014

completo Camagüey
(fully accomplished, literally *all Camagüey*)
—Cuban expression

On our way out of the cafeteria, we stopped to speak to Pinochet, one of the "characters" of the seminary, someone we often ate with when we find a spot at the table with gardeners and grounds crew. An 80-something man with a thin frame and thin hair to match, he hobbles to the seminary each day on one good leg and one prosthesis, with the aid of a single crutch. He lost his right leg years ago when the seminary was clearing land for its organic garden. Like most Cubans engaged in the task of clearing weeds, his only tool had been a machete. He was working alone one afternoon when he fell down a hill, and the machete went deep into his leg. It was several hours before someone found him, and this near-death experience makes him eternally grateful to even be alive. He is always in such a positive spirit, ready with a good word of encouragement for the students and faculty and staff.

While the gardeners and grounds crew left the cafeteria to go back to their tasks, Pinochet did not join them. The fall and his lost limb had signaled the end of his gardening and ground crew days, but not the end of his seminary work. The administration found other employment for him. So there he was, at his usual after-lunch station at a table near the door, meticulously about his job, cleaning the rice for the next meal.

The Cuban expression for this is *escoger el arroz*, that is, *choosing* the rice. To choose the rice, you put a mountain of it on the table, and begin selecting the grains of rice from the tiny stones and other road debris. If you are ever on the carretera near La Vallita after one of the two rice harvests, you will see why this cleaning, or selection, has to be done. The harvested rice is trucked from the paddies to the highway, where it is spread out along the smoothest sections of road to dry, and is then shoveled into large bags. On these days cars and trucks are relegated to the one open lane, the one with more potholes. Whenever there is an oncoming vehicle, the rice unavoidably gets treaded.

Rice drying on the carretera in Camaguey province

Pinochet likes to do the work alone. I suppose it gives him quality time to meditate or reflect on the blessings of life. In most of the other places I have seen, the work is done communally. In La Vallita there is often a small group of women gathered around the table on the back patio, each with her small mountain of rice, doing their selection. It reminded me of my grandmother's era, when she and neighboring women gathered around a quilting frame to do the tedious work of stitching. The process of *escoger el arroz* likewise affords people, generally women, the opportunity to sit and converse and catch up on the news. It is a community-building activity, mindless but essential work with mindful camaraderie, something that I enjoyed whenever given the opportunity. It always brought a smile to the faces of Sila and Anabel, and their neighbors Kari and Hilda and Rafaela, whenever I asked to join them in the ritual.

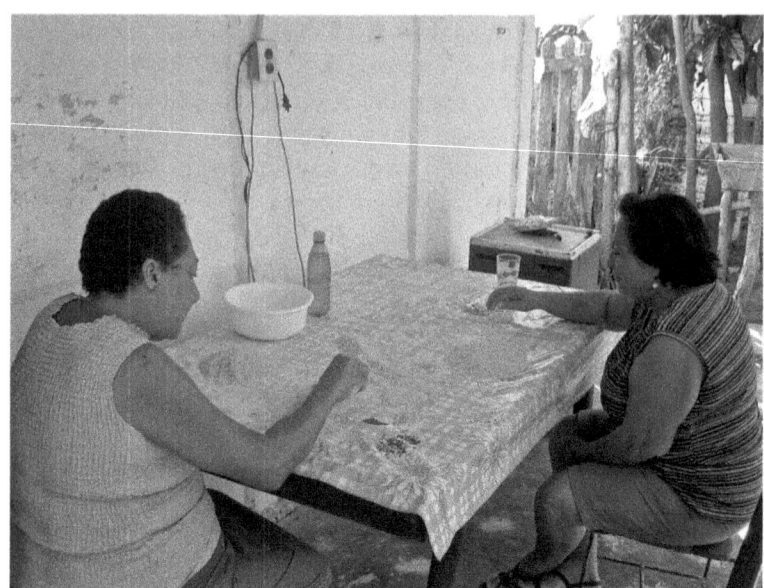

Hilda Cervantes Cervantes and Sila Reyna Cervantes, sorting rice

After greeting Pinochet, I walked with Kim down to the other end of the seminary campus, a scenic overlook where you can sit on the steps in front of the administration building and see the Yumuri River flowing into the bay of Matanzas. Kim always walked here after meals, with some leftover *ave* in hand to share with Niña, the campus rescue dog.

Kim forged many friendships with mutual animal lovers who shared the laments over the sad condition of dogs and cats who wandered the streets. If the reasonably good health and high education of the general populace of Cuba fooled you into thinking that the Revolution really had triumphed over poverty, the animals reminded you otherwise. Some were obviously dying, lying in the shade of a storefront awning with nothing more than patches of mangy fur covering bones, slowly panting their final breaths in the heat. In somewhat better condition were the alpha animals who tended to win the daily battles over bones and table scraps thrown into street gutters.

The sight of these animals occasionally prompted more horror stories of the Special Period, when all of Matanzas' cats disappeared (to show up on the tables of hungry and desperate families) causing the rodent population to flourish. I was happy that the cats had since repopulated and returned to do their jobs, even if their battles over turf and foodstuffs from garbage kept me awake. My sleep was disturbed quite regularly by two felines who had not resolved their alpha-cat conflict, whose cacophonous battle cries would suddenly puncture the calm silence of many a night.

Niña had been rescued from the street after being abandoned as a puppy due to a birth defect, a lame front leg. Her disability did not dissuade her from hobbling gleefully toward Kim whenever she saw her coming, knowing that a treat was in store. After this routine task was fulfilled, I stayed there at the overlook while Kim walked back to foster more animal friendship, this time with the goats who grazed in the grass behind the cafeteria.

Blanquito and Negrito (Whitey and Blackey), like Niña, had learned to anticipate good things when they saw Kim approach. Instead of counting on cafeteria leftovers, though, they enjoyed banana peels and handfuls of green treats from the mint and basil and other herbs proliferating on the edge of the yard. Kim even taught Blanquito a trick, standing up on his hind legs to receive the treat. Having had enough experiences in La Vallita of seeing one's dinner walking around before winding up on the plate, Kim understood that these animals were destined to be part of someone's *fin de año* feast, but she wanted them to enjoy the best life possible while they were being fattened.

Kim and Blanquito

Such ample grazing land like that of the seminary yard is an anomaly in any city, Matanzas included. Most matanceros will get their *carne* from the freezer section of the bodega, except for days like September 28, when the annual celebration marking the birth of the CDRs (Committees for the Defense of the Revolution) includes the butchering of whole hogs as part of block parties. In general, though, seeing one's dinner alive and well up close and personal is more of a rural experience, and marks another difference between the cultures of places like Matanzas and La Vallita.

Anabel, Sila's daughter, butchers hundreds of chickens and pigs each day at the nearby slaughterhouse. I suppose that for some this would have a numbing effect, but for Anabel, I think it has tenderized her heart toward all things living, knowing firsthand as she does what it costs the animal world for humans to have this kind of protein on the table. I never heard from her or anyone else any horror stories of cat meat filling the bellies of hungry La Vallitan families during the Special Period. I suspect that what is true in many places around the world was true in Cuba as well: the country folks fared better in terms of nutrition, even while suffering other scarcities of extreme poverty during the 1990s. Even now, the dogs and cats in the countryside appear to enjoy a more comfortable life, living as they do closer to the food sources that supply the distant cities.

Amaury with Francisca

Amaury, Sila's son, is another tenderhearted animal lover. While his official work has been with cows and goats and pigs his entire adult life, his real love is horses. Several years ago, he dreamed of starting a sustainable micro-enterprise for the church and community, breeding horses for use in transportation. Our church helped fund the project with an investment for them to purchase the initial foal, along with a buggy that would be used to transport people to church as well as to the closest town, Florida, fifteen miles away. It was a wonder to watch him care for Chequira, and see the pride he took as she learned to pull the coach. He bred her, and gave Kim the opportunity to name the new *potrica*. Kim chose to channel the spirit of an ancient animal lover, Saint Francis, christening the newborn with the name Francisca. We enjoyed watching the foal following her mother's every move. Then, we got the heartbreaking news that Chequira had been stolen. Country folk, for all their virtues of good animal husbandry, also are subject to the vice of banditry. Several months of police investigation turned up no clues, leading to the speculation that the horse had been slaughtered for its meat.

The irony is that a similar kind of banditry is rampant now in south Florida, where nostalgic Cuban expats consider horse meat a delicacy and a necessity for their pre-Revolution dish *tasajo*, a stew made with dried jerky of the equine variety. The Hialeah *tasajo* aficionados are willing to pay ten times more for black market horse meat than for beef in order to enjoy this delicacy. It is doubtful that such nostalgia exists among the contemporary La Vallita crowd. The suspicion is Chequira was slaughtered simply to satiate someone's hunger. It came at a great price, in Amaury's broken heart that has yet to heal.

View of Yumuri River and Bay of Matanzas from seminary

Back in the city, it was a clear day, perfect for sitting and gazing at the picturesque Matanzas scene below the overlook, with the sun glistening over the water and broad-winged hawks slowly soaring high overhead, spying out their own brand of carne on which to feast. To the left, across the river, is Versalles, where we had been that morning. Earlier in the year, we could have taken an even shorter cut than the one Julio César led us through, by way of the Marina. We could have simply walked across the Yumuri's footbridge. This bridge, however, had collapsed and was still not repaired. It collapsed one night just hours after we had used it to go visit Lázaro and Tamara. It was the night we had dinner while listening to the music of the Beatles in the style of Gregorian monastery chanting, followed by Kim and Tamara trading dance lessons: tap for salsa.

The walk home over the footbridge was hardly more than ten minutes. Subsequent visits to their house would take much longer. Seeing what was left of the bridge reminded me of the discomfort I always felt in making the trip from Matanzas to Havana, seeing the road signs as we approached the long bridge spanning the Yumurí Valley: *Aviso: Puente en Mal Estado* (Warning: Bridge in Bad Condition). It did not inspire confidence.

From this vantage point I could also see people walking along the tracks of the Hershey Train, another transportation option between Matanzas and Havana. While I harbored romantic notions of riding the rails, partly fueled by reading the biography of Wanda's father, Manuel, seeing his nostalgic descriptions of weekend train rides when he was drawing cartoons for *Juventud Rebelde*, I never summoned the courage to board the fabled train. Too many other stories of breakdowns and people being cooped up for hours and even days waiting on maintenance kept me risking car rides that traversed bad bridges.

The road along the Hershey tracks is, like all the roads in Matanzas, filled with potholes, making it much more practical for pedestrian than motorized traffic. Unlike those in the Blackburn, Lancashire streets from the Beatles' *Day in the Life*, the Cuban potholes are not "rather small," and while I doubt that anyone would have the patience to count the number of Matanzas potholes, my suspicion is there would be considerably more than the 4,000 counted in Lancashire.

This points to another of the contrasts between this western Cuban city and the cities and towns farther to the east. Whenever I asked matanceros why their streets were so much worse than in say, Holguín or Camagüey or Cienfuegos, I generally got one of two responses: the fallback response is to place blame, as with all of Cuba's problems, on the U.S. economic blockade. The other is a response of contempt toward incompetent government leadership. Even people who had served in the *Poder Popular* (the People's Power) local governance voiced some of this disgust. Whichever the cause, and I suspect the true culprit is a mixture of both the blockade and a failure of local leadership, it is evident that the deferred maintenance and disintegration of infrastructure, while experienced at some level in all parts of Cuba, is more severe and acute in Matanzas.

I am waiting for someone in the city to coin a phrase similar to *completo Camagüey* that could describe the phenomenon. The Camagüey expression, which has come to mean anything that is fulfilled completely, originated in the early months of revolutionary rule, when Castro's leaders turned the city of Camagüey into a showcase for how to thoroughly take over all private enterprise and fully eradicate all counterrevolutionary cell groups. It was a slam dunk, a model for how to get things done. The Matanzas expression should refer instead to the general sense of failure that, if not complete, is predominant among the frustrated matanceros.

Maybe the new phrase could be *mayormente Matanzas*. Anywhere in the country, someone could voice their frustration at not being able to get something done by saying *mainly Matanzas*. The city's relative lack of ability to pour asphalt into a hole is further evidence in support of my working theory that the greater the dissent of any particular community, the less likely it is that any frustration will easily be resolved. So the cars drive slowly through town, dodging each hole and taking all sorts of detours to avoid the worst patches.

As I watched people walking the Versalles roads, I thought about Lázaro and Tamara and the walks they make on these roads every day. They are among Kim's kindred spirit compassionate animal lovers, counting their pet dog Mya as a bona fide family member. I never learned the story behind how the blue-eyed Mya came to their home. She is a large, long-haired husky-type breed that could not have been bred for the Cuban climate, but I do know that she is one of the most beloved and well-cared for (maybe I should say "spoiled") creatures in Matanzas. I also know that Lázaro and Tamara are among the most compassionate people I have ever met. They take advantage of the daily walks to notice things, to pay attention, not only to the four-legged creatures, but to their neighbors in need.

Lázaro has a question that he has asked more than one North American visitor, *Is it true what I have heard, that in the U.S. it's possible for someone not to know their neighbors?* The reply is generally the same, *Yes, it's probably more of the norm*. Which prompts Lázaro to ask a follow-up question, *Then how do people survive?* This is more of a rhetorical question, as there is not a good answer that would make sense to him in his context. For Lázaro, keeping your eyes open as you walk the streets, paying attention to the neighbors who tread the same path as you, is not just a matter of having good values. It is the way you collectively survive in a system not designed for individual winners and losers.

Lázaro is a light-skinned, thin and thinly mustached painter and sculptor, as well as composer and musician. He is also a mystic who has a keen eye for the deep beauty and sacred spirit alive and at work in every setting, including his dilapidating neighborhood which on the surface lacks aesthetic attraction. Tamara, an attractive, medium-built *mulatta* (a commonly-used racial identifier in Cuba) who loves to dance, shares the spiritual mystic eye (and hers almost always has a glimmer in it). She sees the potential for beauty, perhaps not so much on a canvas, but in the relationships they forge within their surroundings.

Tamara and Lázaro

As I sat there at the seminary overlook watching people walk along the Versalles roads, I reflected again on one story of theirs that blew me away, an experience that exemplifies the depth of their compassion. A couple of years prior, Tamara had been on her daily walk to the various bodegas and particulares in search of dinner fare, when she noticed an elderly woman sitting in her doorway, disheveled, talking to herself. Tamara stopped to speak to the woman, and then made a habit of stopping each day to check on her.

Every evening at the dinner table Tamara would recount to Lázaro and their son Lazarito (then in his late teens) and daughter Yeni María (around 7 years old) what had happened with the elderly woman that day. These narratives continued for around two weeks, increasing in intensity of need and compassion care. It started with the simple sharing of bread. Then upon discovering that the woman did not have food in the pantry, Tamara began preparing lunch for her each day. Next came laundering clothes, and when Tamara noticed that the clean clothes did not mask the body odor, she started bathing her.

These daily stories continued until Tamara finally asked the family if they were prepared to receive a new family member in the home, so she could properly care for her. Mind you, there was not a spare room, but this did not dissuade her. Nor did it deter the family, for her stories had prepared them well. They were not phased in the least bit when Tamara suggested that Yeni María could sleep in her and Lázaro's room, so that the new family member could have Yeni's bed.

Tamara and Yeni María

Tamara had learned from other neighbors that the 90-plus year-old woman was widowed, and her only daughter had died some years earlier. Her sole surviving relative was an estranged half-sister with whom she had not spoken for years. The woman was obviously suffering from some kind of dementia, and in her confused state began thinking that Tamara was her daughter, calling her by her daughter's name, Yadira.

The whole family showered the old woman with affection. Yeni María treated her as a beloved grandmother, and would comb her hair every day, saying, *Abuela, you have the most beautiful hair*. Tamara played the role of Yadira well, loving her as she would have her own mother. All this tender care had a healing effect on the woman's confused mind. As the months went by, she began regaining her faculties. She understood that Tamara was not Yadira, and this was not her biological family. More than two years into her stay, she had her own announcement to make. She told them that her body was failing her, that she was dying. She knew it in her bones. She expressed great appreciation for the wonderful compassion Tamara and family had shown her. But, she said, she had a desire to go home. She wanted to die in her own home, in her own bed.

Tamara understood, but was not comfortable thinking about the woman living alone. So she began searching for the woman's estranged half-sister, found her, and began a process of reconciliation between the two. While she was doing this, Lázaro and the others were hard at work cleaning and fixing up the home for her return. At last the time came, and the woman went home, with her sister moving in as her caretaker. Lázaro and Tamara and the kids continued visiting until the woman died, just two weeks after returning home. She died happy, content, at peace, surrounded by love in familiar surroundings.

The name *Versalles* has a Latin etymology that means to keep turning, to continue plowing the ground, preparing the soil for new seeds to be sown. Even in a city where the cynicism runs deep and there are severe doubts that anything good can ever be accomplished, Lázaro and Tamara keep turning the soil, preparing their land for something new. They refuse to be locked in to despair, and choose instead to be part of the solution for whatever problems emerge on their pockmarked streets. If the Revolution had its *completo Camagüey* and the critics of the Revolution have their *mayormente Matanzas*, this barrio has a family working to make it a *Verdadero Versalles*, a true turning, a real revolution.

Chapter Fifteen

2:00 P.M. – Children

I saw the photograph.
–Lennon/McCartney

It's time for a new approach.
–President Obama, December 17, 2104

¿y ahora qué?
(and now what?)
–Cuban expression

Senator Patrick Leahy, speaking on NBC's Today Show, reflected on the work he had done for Gerardo Hernández before his release, making it possible for the prisoner and his spouse to fulfill a dream: *We just did it as a human thing. I think it impressed the Cubans. ...And then we got a letter from her, saying that she was pregnant, and thanking us so very much. I mean, I feel like the godfather or something in this. I've never met her husband, but I've seen the pictures since they reunited, the joy on his face, especially the joy on hers, and they're going to have a little girl.*

Not many people in Cuba would have suspected that Gerardo Hernández would be greeted by a very pregnant spouse, Adriana Pérez, upon his arrival home after being released from a U.S. prison that Wednesday morning. Not to worry, the Hero had no concerns over paternity, for "godfather" Patrick Leahy and others had intervened on the prisoner's behalf to give him a chance for fatherhood. The intervention was not for conjugal visits. That would be too much to ask, given the embargo. What the Vermont Senator was able to do was gain clearance for a long-distance artificial insemination project, funded by the Cuban government and facilitated by one of Leahy's staffers. A *Democracy Now* podcast would cleverly title the saga "The Diplomaculate Conception."

I only learned of the couple's happy news three weeks later, when the *Granma* announced the birth of Gema (in English, "Gem") Hernández Pérez on its front page, complete with photograph of baby girl and proud parents. Weighing in at a healthy seven pounds, seven ounces, Gema came into this world and made her *epiphany* (striking appearance), appropriately enough, on Epiphany, January 6, *el día de los tres magos*. Three Kings Day is the day of Christmas gift-giving in the Latin American liturgical calendar. As the *Granma* put it, this "gem" was the fruit of love, the perfect gift for a couple who for sixteen years survived the distance of unjust incarceration.

Even without knowing this bit of world news, by the afternoon of that Wednesday we all sensed that we were living in a historically significant time. Kim sometimes has a peculiar way of celebrating those significant times. Before getting to my task for the afternoon (learning wedding music for the following day), I walked back across the seminary campus to find her, and there she was, with Blanquito the goat in tow, visiting the seminary's manger scene.

Kim with Blanquito and seminary manger scene

This was the only such sacred lawn adornment that existed in Matanzas as far as I knew. It was a simple scene, by U.S. extravagant light show standards. A star hovered over the small hut sheltering Mary and Joseph, who knelt over the manger cradling the baby Jesus. This unembellished scene (apart from the temporary adornment of foreigner and goat joining the holy family) had its attraction though, as a fairly steady stream of matancero parents brought children throughout the days of Advent to stand in front of the crèche in adoration. The families who were there that particular day did not seem to mind Kim's bringing Blanquito along. Perhaps she and the goat were seen as stand-ins for the shepherds and their flocks.

As much as our culture has co-opted the Christmas narrative for consumer interests, there is still something exceptional about the story of a child of promise coming unexpectedly to a young unwed woman of color and her handyman of a husband on the margins of an empire. I could not help reflect on the exceptionality of all children of promise who come, expected or not, to Cuban parents.

The very act of bearing a child has increasingly become the exception to the rule in this country where the birth rate is in free fall. Birth control is free and accessible, and an "interruption" of pregnancy (their word for abortion, whether natural or induced) does not carry the stigma that it does in our culture. Because of these and other factors, Cuba has a demographic crisis on its hands, with a rapidly growing senior sector of the population and a rapidly declining youth sector. While Cormac McCarthy and the Coen brothers might describe our nation as "No Country for Old Men," Cubans seem to be dramatically proclaiming in deed if not word that their nation is no country for babies.

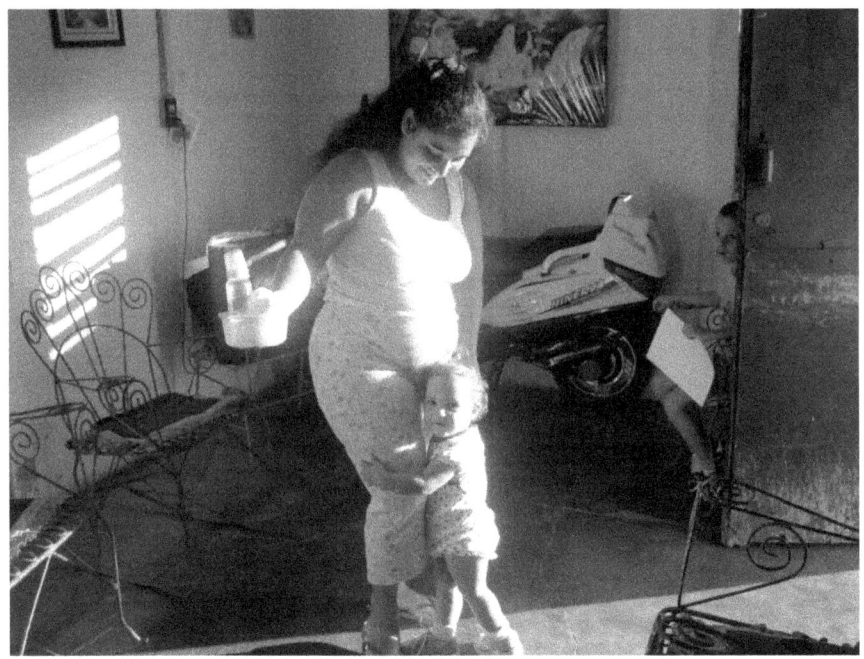

Anabel with Lisy

If all you did was read and analyze these demographics, you might expect to visit Cuba and have very little interaction with babies and preschoolers. What I have loved about being there over the years has been encountering so many exceptions to the statistical rule. Even in our first visits in the Special Period of despair, parents were defying the traditional wisdom and were giving birth. Preschoolers abounded, and it has been a joy to watch them grow and develop over these two decades. We have been blessed to participate with Sila in several baby dedications there in the church, for her two youngest grandchildren, Lisy and Norly, among others. We have also been there enough to see how the adage of an entire village raising children is definitely embodied in that community. All hands are on deck.

The challenges of bringing up babies and ensuring they hit all their developmental marks are indeed daunting in this environment, given the gravity of daily economic struggles. Despite all odds and demographic trends, though, these recalcitrant parents are defying gravity. I can imagine them getting the positive test results confirming a pregnancy, and responding with the oft-heard expression, *¿Y ahora qué? (And now what?)* They ask the rhetorical question and then put hand to the plow to be about the business of birthing and child-rearing.

This defiance does not just happen in the countryside. We were surrounded by little ones in Matanzas, as well. The seminary was playground for the little tykes of students and staff. We delighted in seeing the preschoolers at play: Darjel's twin boys imitating pirates outside of chapel, using the long, curved seed pods of the flamboyán tree for their swords. Little Betsabet alongside Victor, her dad, serving up coffee for meriendas. Isis picking flowers for a bouquet for her mom, Alicita. Farfán and Ania's daughter Marina singing nursery rhymes. Kids from the neighborhood frolicking on the swing set.

I never asked any of the parents, but I did often wonder: what was the font of their defiance, their courage, their resilience, in choosing to bring up children in this society that so many, according to the stats, were finding insupportable? I know of many who chose differently, who made the move to the greener pastures of Europe or the U.S. or Canada, to raise children in environments with different sets of challenges. I understand and respect those who find that the Cuban wells have gone dry or the water is no longer potable, who launch out in search of living water, but their stories only serve to put the images of those who have chosen to stay in stark relief. It is this kind of exceptionality that fascinates me, the defiant faith that caused Sila and her community to name their church *Rivers of Living Water* and to live and act in a way that tells you they really believe it.

It is this kind of resiliency that creates so much celebration when there is news of a pregnancy, no matter the circumstance. The wedding shower for our seminary student for whom we were to play music turned out to be a baby shower as well. No stigma, no judgment, just joy and celebration. We met that Wednesday afternoon to finalize the song selections for the following day's service, and I was happy that *Ave María* got switched out. I am more of a *Wind Cries Mary* kind of musician. I was also happy that the songs that did make the cut had a good bit of North American influence regarding melody and style, so I would not worry about my *yuma* rhythms showing through too much and clashing with the singer.

It was not only the parents and soon-to-be parents who were defying the demographic message that Cuba is no place to raise a child. The joy and anticipation of birth was matched by the hopes and sometimes griefs of those who were struggling with infertility challenges. We were able to share our own story and resonate with a seminary couple who had been through a fertility clinic experience, and were weighing whether to give it another try. We remembered one of our early trips to Cuba, when we befriended a pastor and his spouse who were trying and hoping as we were. We covenanted to pray for one another. They now have two children, a 12-year-old son and 9-year-old daughter, whom Kim taught English during our year. The joy of their answered prayer mingled with the tender places of disappointment that still linger for us.

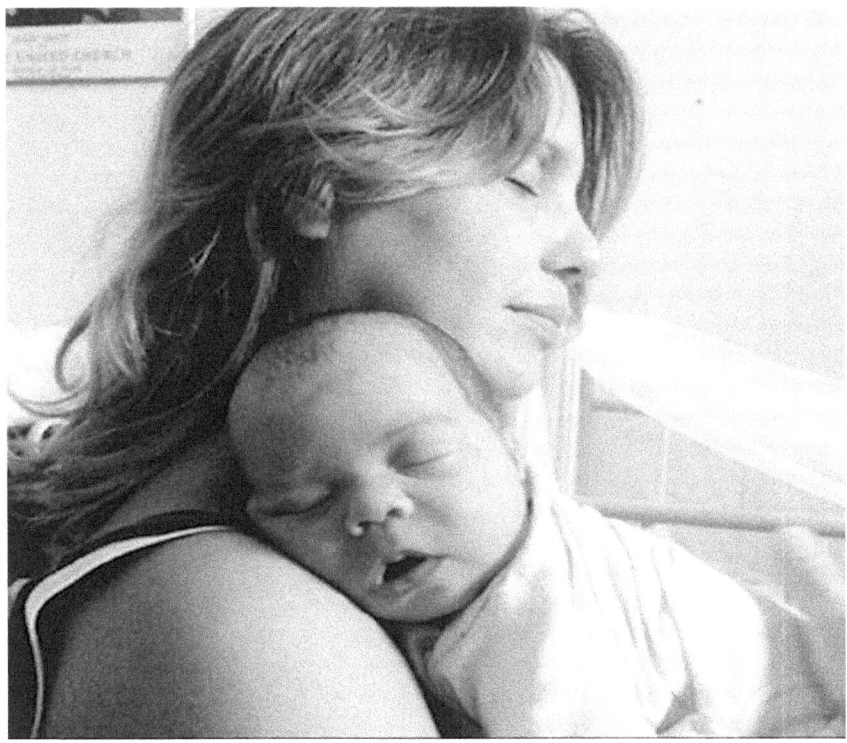

Wanda with Lucas, photo by Ingrid Fundora Hernández

At the time I am writing this, a package just arrived in the mail, in time for Kim to carry as Christmas presents on a trip back to Cuba she will be taking in a couple of weeks. They are Star Wars themed onesies, to give to Wanda and Orestes. We knew during our year there that they had been trying for some time to get pregnant. They announced their good news about the time the country learned of Gerardo's good news of fatherhood. Orestes is a big fan of Star Wars, so when teenager Ingrid and her friends suggested the name Lucas for her little brother-to-be, Orestes consented, on the condition that the middle name be Skywalker. The onesies say, "I am a Jedi, like my father."

The joy of this recent birth is balanced with another grief, though, as we learned today that little Lucas' grandfather, Orestes' father, suffered a severe stroke and passed away this morning. Maybe it is because Orestes and I share such a love of rock music, but I could not help hearing the lyrics of the Blood Sweat and Tears song when I heard the news: *And when I die, and when I'm gone, there'll be one child born in this world to carry on... All I ask of living is to have no chains on me. All I ask of dying is to go naturally.* My impression of Papo, Orestes' father, was that he lived his life freely, unchained, despite whatever political structures or strictures surrounded him, and he died naturally. I hope this can be solace to the family as they now ask the inevitable question, *¿y ahora qué?*

Part Four

Connections, Confections, and Conjectures

3:00 P.M. - 8:00 P.M.

Chapter Sixteen

3:00 P.M. – Friends and Family

I went upstairs.
–Lennon/McCartney

This is fundamentally about freedom and openness, and also expresses my belief in the power of people-to-people engagement.
–President Obama, December 17, 2014

Antes de morirme quiero echar mis versos de alma.
(Before I die I hope to bestow the verses of my soul.)
–from José Martí's most famous poem

The news of Papo's death made my heart ache for Orestes and Wanda, who must have harbored dreams of little Lucas growing up on his granddad's knees. I lamented that I could not travel there to be with my Cuban family for the funeral. It takes around three months to get all the visa paperwork processed, and the general practice for Cubans is to have the service and the burial the day after the death. Maybe one day the travel bureaucracy will change, and day-of tickets will be available.

I am writing this chapter one year to the day after the big newsflash of renewed diplomacy, and perhaps in commemoration of that anniversary, the government has announced that commercial airlines will soon be allowed to offer service to Havana, replacing the complicated system of charter flights. I doubt the bureaucratic process of visas will get shorter any time soon, though, so when it comes to loss of loved ones, we will continue having to send our thoughts and prayers and hugs and messages of consolation from afar.

When I got word a few days ago that Papo had suffered a stroke, the news took me back almost a year to the day, when we got similar news of Kim's dad and our need for a travel miracle to get home quickly. It would be miraculous, but not impossible, because the bureaucracy of travel from Cuba to the U.S. is much less cumbersome. It was around 3:00, and as we were finishing up the wedding music preparations, one of the seminary custodians found us to say that we needed to call Kim's sister. There was a family emergency. We suspected that it had something to do with Kim's father.

Ed had suffered a stroke a month earlier, causing partial paralysis on one side. Kim had flown home to be with him for a couple of weeks. The prognosis was hopeful. He had some initial positive responses to the physical therapy. She had felt a great deal of weight over the question of if and when to return to Cuba, but when she talked with her dad about it, he did not hesitate. She had to return. In this conversation, he was clear, showing no signs of the dementia and confusion that had plagued many conversations for several months. He tapped into his old core self to assure her that he was in good care, that he was proud of the work she was doing. He sat up straight and tall and said that it was important to him and to her mom that she carry on with that work. When Kim confessed her feeling of guilt, her dad was adamant that she need feel no such thing. *Not even a drop?* she asked. *Not even half a drop*, was his answer

There was no doubt that he was under the best care imaginable. Kim's mom had been a genius at retirement planning, starting early in their married life, plus she had the foresight to invest in long-term health insurance, all of which enabled them to enjoy the sunset years in Salemtowne, a Moravian retirement facility with graduated care for assisted living and health care needs. The last time that Paco Rodés, retired pastor and founder of the Kairos Center, visited us, we took him to visit Kim's parents, and he was amazed by the comforts of Salemtowne, likening it to one of the finest resort hotels in Varadero Beach. Having some knowledge of the *hogares de ancianos* (old folks' homes) in Cuba, I could understand his sense of wonder, and the contrast created one of those awkward embarrassments of riches for us.

Kim's ability to travel and see about her dad's condition also gave us a twinge of embarrassment, or a half-drop of guilt, as we compared our family dynamics to those of many Cubans. Paco's family is a case in point. His two daughters are both exiles, living in Atlanta, welcomed to our country as refugees from, as the Cuban Adjustment Act describes it, political oppression. They have shared with us the tremendous weight they and others like them carry. Leaving behind parents who do not share the sense of being persecuted, who choose to age in a country with bare-bones resources for senior care, creates more than a drop of guilt. Neither the blessing of the parents, the regular remittances, nor the occasional visits are enough to assuage the self-reproach of children living under the asylum of our country.

Our suspicions were validated when we got through to Kim's sister, and learned that Ed had suffered another stroke. The doctors did not give hope of recovery, and did not give him long to live. They could not say with certainty, but thought it would be a matter of days, not weeks. We found out from HavanaTour, the one agency you have to deal with to get plane tickets, that there was little chance of making it back anytime soon. Being Christmas season, all flights were completely sold out until after the new year. The best we could do was put our name on a waiting list.

Needing some prayers, I used the rest of our domestic calling card to phone Sila. She assured us of her prayers and those of the church family. She had fallen in love with Kim's parents when we took her there for a visit a year earlier, and I knew we could count on her to lift up the whole family and hold us all in the light. After hanging up, we then shared the troubling news with the seminary custodians before going upstairs to our seminary apartment to try to breathe, settle our nerves, and get to the business of planning what to do next.

On our way upstairs we ran into our neighbor Farfán, the facilities director for the seminary. He was the ideal neighbor, being the go-to guy for anything that needed fixing or replacing. He was excellent at his job, but I came to suspect that his hidden desire was to be a gourmet chef in a great restaurant. Some weekends we had the good fortune of sampling some of his exquisite creations. Before going into our apartment we filled him in on what was happening. As a born doer, he was quick to assure us that if there was anything he could do, to let him know. We would later take him up on his offer, as he was able to get us a ride to the airport.

We had not long settled in when there was a knock at the door. We looked up to see Daniel Montoya, longtime seminary chaplain and theology professor. (We had learned the Cuban practice of keeping our door open, which created both airflow and a sense of community.) The news of our situation had quickly spread, and Montoya, as he was affectionately known, simply wanted to come and sit with us for a while. Kim's dad had also been a university chaplain, and he and Montoya were cut from the same cloth, with a quick wit, contagious sense of humor, and wisdom about how to offer pastoral care. Add to that a steel trap memory.

For Montoya, the memory bank contained hundreds of poems and lyrics. He was always (notoriously) ready with a verse or song appropriate for whatever occasion. As much as any Cuban, I think Montoya embodies the simple verse of José Martí, immortalized in *Guantanamera*, Cuba's most famous song: *Antes de morirme quiero echar mis versos de alma. (Before I die I hope to bestow the verses of my soul.)* On this afternoon I asked him to repeat the story he had shared in class, about the Revolutionary hero Frank País. This founder of the clandestine July 26 movement was the son of a Baptist pastor, and Montoya had been a member of their church. He teared up talking about how after País was murdered, someone in the church composed an elegy, a hymn in his honor.

Daniel Montoya

We then talked about Montoya's spouse, Ofelia Ortega, who was away at the People's Assembly, of which she is one of the three evangelical Christian leaders serving. I inquired about her health. A recent bout with bronchitis and laryngitis revealed to us just how lacking in resources the highly touted and effective Cuban health system is. The last time Montoya had knocked on our door had been the previous weekend. Ofelia had been doctoring a persistent cough with home remedies, to no avail. Her doctor prescribed an antibiotic, but there was none to be found in any of the Matanzas pharmacies, not even for a member of the Assembly.

Ordinarily they would have continued the alternative herbal treatments, but Ofelia needed to get her voice back soon. She and her fellow evangelical Christian deputies to the Assembly, Raúl Suárez and Oden Marichal, were due to speak to their fellow deputies on the role of the Church in the betterment of Cuban society. She had been excited for several weeks about this opportunity to promote the important role the Church had been playing in fostering the ideals of the Revolution. Montoya had inquired on that earlier visit whether we might have an antibiotic in our personal pharmacy (which he knew that most *yumas* bring along, just in case). We did, and it worked. She recovered her voice just in time and could well have been speaking to the *Asamblea* right as we conversed.

We were happy to imagine that we had done our part to further the life of the Church in Cuba, giving Ofelia an opportunity to share the stage with Raúl and Oden to address the legislators. It was quite the ecumenical trio, Presbyterian (Ofelia), Baptist (Raúl), and Episcopalian (Oden). Montoya laughed as I shared with him a story of the Baptist of the bunch, Raúl Suárez, who in the 1990s had been the first Christian leader elected to this national office. Reverend Suárez has always impressed me with his unbounded energy. Along with legislating, he had been pastor of Ebenezer Baptist and Director of the Martin Luther King Center in *Maríanao*, a seminary professor, and member of Cuba's Council of Churches. At 80 years old, he is retired from most of these duties, but continues in his role as Center Director, and preaches on occasion. You can count on a Raúl Suárez sermon to be fiery and prophetic.

Back to the story I was sharing with Daniel Montoya: A month or so prior I had been the guest preacher at Ebenezer, where Raúl is now pastor emeritus. I confessed to the chaplain that my ego had taken over. I wanted to take my A-game, being aware that this hero of the faith would be in the congregation. I thought I did well enough, and got an ego-boosting affirmation after the service, when Raúl made his way to me and gave me a big hug, thanked me, and asked if I would send him a copy of the sermon. My ego quickly deflated, though, when he added, *My hearing aids are not working well, and I could not hear a word you were saying.*

Soon after Montoya left, yet another knock came to the door, and we welcomed Paco Rodés into our abode. I put some coffee on, knowing how much Paco loves it. He inquired about the condition of Kim's dad, and on hearing the news sighed a simple *ay caramba* (oh no). We sat for a while, not needing to punctuate the silence with Paco. It is good to have friends like that, because we were at the point where words were likely to bring tears, and we were not quite ready to break down. At some point Kim asked Paco if he would voice a prayer for us, and he did. Paco, like his fellow prison chaplain Lázaro, is something of a mystic, drawing from a deep well of spirituality that gives tremendous weight to his words.

I remembered the time I had interviewed Paco some years earlier for my "separated at birth" project, dual sets of interviews with Cubans and U.S. folks who shared similar life's work. I had asked each pair the same sets of questions, about what drew them into their vocation, who influenced them, etc. Paco had talked about the influence of the Catholic monk Thomas Merton, a French-born mystic from New York who had received his call to monastic life as a Trappist while on a pilgrimage in Cuba. When I asked the same questions to Paco's U.S. counterpart in the project, Mahan Siler, he, too, counted Merton as one of his prime influences. On that particular afternoon, as we sat there with Paco, not knowing what to do, having trouble imaging what the next days would hold, one of Merton's oft-quoted prayers helped us surrender some of our anxiety and trust that all would be well: *Lord God, I have no idea where I am going. I do not see the road ahead of me. I cannot know for certain where it will end. Nor do I really know myself, and the fact that I think that I am following your will does not mean that I am actually doing so. But I believe that the desire to please you does in fact please you.*

Francisco "Paco" Rodés

When Paco was ready to leave, we walked out with him, and our stroll across the grounds brought many more well-wishes and hugs and inquiries, from students, faculty, gardeners, cleaners. Paco's sister-in-law, Chavela, the Administrative Assistant to the seminary President, assured us that we would get a flight. She put us in touch with Moraima, who handles all the travel logistics for church groups from Canada and the U.S. coming to visit the seminary. Moraima encouraged us, saying that while she could not give any guarantees, she was going to do her best to get us home before Christmas. If we could be at the airport first thing Monday morning, she would work her contacts and get us seats sometime that week. Even as we trusted her, we knew it was a long shot, as there are only a handful of charter flights leaving Havana any given day.

We eventually became convinced that Moraima was part of a network of angels. When we arrived at the airport Monday morning, we were greeted by HavanaTour agents who escorted us through the maze of travel chaos into an inner office, where another agent let us know we were going to soon be home. She also let us know she was a person of faith, and would be praying for us. For Cubans, this is something of a secret handshake, as government workers in the public eye, such as the HavanaTour folks, still feel some of the residue of those long years when the country was officially atheistic and people of faith were prohibited from holding many jobs. This has not been the case for twenty-five years, but the shadows of the discrimination still loom large across the workplace. So the faithful make connections in whispered tones. This particular agent went to work on her outdated computer, and it was not long before she looked up and said if we were ready, she could get us on a flight in an hour and a half.

Given the long, long passages of bureaucracy that always accompany any travel planning, it is hard to overstate what a shock this angel's message was. *Fear not, you are headed home.* We were indeed packed and ready, bags in hand. She escorted us through security to the gate, and we were soon on board. We arrived at Salemtowne that evening and had a tender visit with Kim's dad. Though he was not responsive, we trusted that he knew of our presence. Kim had brought her dulcimer, and the next day we played Christmas carols for her mom and dad and the nurses attending him. He passed early the next morning, Christmas Eve, the day after their sixty-third anniversary.

Scores of people came to Ed's funeral. While none of our Cuban family were able to be at the service, we felt their presence in a powerful way. It occurred to me that even though Ed did not speak Spanish, and would not have known the works of José Martí, he, like Daniel Montoya, surely embodied that simple line, *Antes de morirme quiero echar mis versos de alma.* Before I die I hope to bestow the verses of my soul. We returned to Cuba some days after the funeral, carrying many verses of Ed's soul song along with us.

Chapter Seventeen

4:00 P.M. – Technology

A crowd of people turned away.
–Lennon/McCartney

As we have reiterated, we must learn the art of coexisting with our differences in a civilized manner.
–President Castro, December 17, 2014

¿La última?
(Who's the last in line?)
–Cuban expression

We made the call home to learn of Ed's situation on the last of our international phone cards. We had decided early on to go low-tech for our year, which meant not investing in a cell phone, even though they were becoming more common, at least in the cities. I cannot remember our reasoning, other than being stingy with our budget. There is a great Cuban expression for people like us who pinch pennies–*andar por los codos*–walking on your elbows (presumably to save shoe leather). Perhaps another motivation was to be more in solidarity with Sila and the folks in La Vallita, who got by well enough without a mobile phone. Knowing that afternoon that we would need to make more calls home, I headed back to town to pay a visit to Etecsa, Cuba's state-run telecommunications enterprise, to buy more calling cards.

As I left campus I ran into Duvier, one of the seminary gardeners, who inquired about Kim and her dad. Kim, being the egregious extrovert and goodhearted person she is, had really endeared herself to the entire seminary community, but she really made a lasting connection with the gardeners. She made a commitment early on to spend every Friday morning in the garden, pulling weeds or doing whatever there was to be done on a given day. This struck a chord with the guys who did this on a daily basis, because they had become somewhat invisible to the rest of the seminary community. On one occasion, Ofelia Ortega voiced a prayer concern about this in chapel, speaking about how the seminary had become divided, between the academicians–students and faculty–and the nonacademic side of campus, that is, the workers. Ofelia had a vision of it being one united, beloved community. Kim was in a very real way modeling an answer to Ofelia's prayer.

Kim and I both had formed a particular bond with Duvier, partly because we knew his history. I became acquainted with him several years earlier, when I was there one October and helped lead a concert in the park in honor of John Lennon's birthday. Duvier, a gentle, quiet man, with long gray hair braided in a ponytail, rode his bike several miles to be there for the concert (more of a sing-along). Orestes and Julio César later shared some of his story with me. He had been part of Cuba's underground rock music scene back in the 1980s and 90s, a drummer for a heavy metal group called Sectarium. His life fell apart after the lead singer of the band was murdered after an underground club show. Alcoholism took over Duvier's life, and he bottomed out before finding redemption through an AA program run by the First Baptist Church, which eventually led to his being employed by the seminary.

Duvier with Kim

After Ofelia's prayer for more community and solidarity on campus, I gave my class an assignment. I scanned a photo of a much younger and shirtless and dark-haired Duvier playing the drums, and showed it to the students, telling them that someone among the campus community had once been a hard rocker in the underground movement. Their assignment was to find out who it was and interview him, finding out what that period was like, what the group's message was, and what the challenges were.

The students went about their search with great curiosity, and once they discovered Duvier, they began to get to know him. They were astounded to find out what the group's message was: the members of Sectarium were all avid readers, and were particularly caught up in the works of Dante Alighieri. For them, his works proved to be a good platform for reflecting critically on the challenges of life in Cuban society. The *Divine Comedy* formed the basis of their impossible-to-understand shouted lyrics. More evidence of the theology of the absurd at work in Cuban society.

After this rock drummer-turned-gardener quietly gave me his best wishes for Kim and her family, I headed down the hill of Dos de Mayo Street, where the usual gaggle of kids was playing stickball and soccer, some shooting marbles, and others spinning tops. If you did not know better you would think you were in a Norman Rockwell painting of street life in the 1950s, before parents became frightened to let their kids play unsupervised on a city street. One of the kids gave the typical greeting whenever a foreigner was passing, using the two words of English everyone had memorized, *my friend!* followed by *dame un fula allí* (give me some real money there. *Fula* refers to any currency that is not the Cuban peso). They laughed as I responded, *¿Qué fula fulano? Soy matancero como tu* (What money, dude? I'm from Matanzas like you).

Boys playing soccer on Matanzas Street

I crossed Contreras Street, where you can always find a game of dominos on the corner, with four men sitting on the sidewalk, holding the tabletop on their knees. I came to love the sound of dominos being scattered or thrown down on a board. I paused to watch one move, hearing a man make the clever word play as he placed a five on the board: *cin-co-mer no puedes vivir* (*cinco* = five, *sin comer* = without eating, *no puedes vivir* = you cannot live). I made the left turn on Milanes to get to Etecsa. This took me through Liberty Park, where I was hailed, as I often was, by Armando.

A thin, cigarette-smoking older man with ragged clothes that give him the look of a street beggar, Armando is one of the treasures of Matanzas, in my view. *Antes* (*before*—this one word is all Cubans need to say when referring to pre-1959, pre-Revolution society), *antes* Armando had been a successful jazz composer, having some of his boleros played by orchestras and sung by torch singers in the resort hotels and clubs of Varadero.

By the time I met Armando, he was hanging out in the park, usually in the shade on the steps of the library, and he was still composing. These days his compositions are handwritten on whatever scrap of cardboard he can find. I have a growing collection of these, as he often wanted to give me one. For "payment" I would treat him to a cafeicito at one of the nearby family coffee shops, where I would prompt him to tell me some stories from back in the day, when his sheet music was on the band stand. On this particular afternoon, I did not have time to indulge in more coffee or conversation, so I begged for a rain check and kept walking toward Etecsa.

Every Cuban city and town has an Etecsa store and office. This is where people go to pay phone bills, buy a cell phone, an internet card to use on one of the six desktop computers, phone cards, or to use the pay phone. Yes, Cuba still has pay phones, making me think that if there is ever a remake of *The Matrix*, they will need to set it in Cuba, given Neo's need for pay phone escape routes. All these services offered in one store meant there was always a line. I usually budgeted an hour of my time whenever going to Etecsa, as this was the average wait. Sometimes (on rare occasion) I got right in, other times not so lucky.

Once I arrived around 5:00 in the afternoon (Etecsa closed at 7:00) to find close to a hundred people in line. There was a special sale on the mobile service, a two-for-one I think, creating more demand than supply for the short-staffed store. The Etecsa manager came out before closing time to inform the hopefuls that they were not going to be served, but not to worry, the sale would be extended another day. A couple of folks in line took it upon themselves to create a list, complete with names and id numbers, for use in re-creating the line the following morning when the store reopened. I wondered if we would find such courtesy and order outside the door of Apple stores when the latest IPhone hits the market.

On the afternoon of December 17, luck was with me, as I only had about a thirty-minute wait to purchase the phone cards. The "line" was not exactly a line, with people congregating in small groups taking advantage of shady spots. I called out the obligatory question, *¿la última?* and took my place next to the person who raised a hand, the last to arrive. As often happened, the "line" was populated by as many foreigners as Cubans. There was a German couple, several Korean medical students, and a Brit, all there to grab some internet from the bank of desktop computers. Foreign visitors have a hard time weaning themselves off of Facebook and email, and come to Etecsa for their screen time connections.

I did some old-school, low-tech reading while waiting in line, preparing for a Bible study I was to lead with the SOMOS lgbt group at the church on Saturday night. I was honing in on the Advent story of Joseph learning of Mary's pregnancy, and his decision to "put her away privately" (being a just man). It occurred to me that this was the first case of civil disobedience in the New Testament, as the Hebrew law mandated that a jealous husband subject the wife under suspicion to a very public, very humiliating and potentially deadly trial. For the cause of justice, Matthew's gospel tells us, Joseph decided to disobey God's word from the law of Moses and keep the whole affair private. I figured that would make for an interesting conversation with the faithful of SOMOS, who for the cause of justice were also defying similar Levitical laws in their sexual expression.

The foreigners around me in line were all reading away on their tablets. The Cubans were conversing, about work, about sports, about music, about the news of the day. I wondered how long this art of conversation and civil discourse, long lost in our culture, would last here, once the new technology took over. The coming days and weeks would bring us news that in the new diplomacy between our two countries, one of the primary strategic goals of the U.S. negotiators was to bring broadband internet and social media to the Cuban populace, of which only a small percentage had access.

It did not take long for the techies to make progress toward this goal. We arrived back in the U.S. in June, six months after the December announcement. Within days, I received around fifty Facebook friend requests from people in Matanzas and Havana, and in no time I was plugged into their personal lives, knowing how they were feeling by way of the same animated emoticons and silly status updates I have always scrolled through on my news feed. I hear now that Matanzas youth are crowding into a corner of Liberty Park every night, so they can swipe some free Wi-Fi from the nearby Hotel Velasco, without having to enter the lobby and buy the requisite drink from the bar.

I am sure that our diplomats are basing this technological strategy on the premise that social media will not simply be a platform for silliness and narcissism, but will fuel dissent and build a movement that will lead to radical reforms, if not outright regime change. That was the thought process behind the half-baked USAID scheme that landed Alan Gross in prison. He had been carrying high-tech equipment for the Cuban dissenters to use in setting up a Twitter-like system of communication, in hopes of fomenting a "smart mob" that would fuel a "Cuban Spring" similar to the Arab Spring uprisings. In their attempts to be clever in the process, the secret agent men called the faux Twitter service ZunZuneo (*zunzun* is the Spanish word for hummingbird). It garnered around forty thousand subscribers before it was outed and blocked by the Cuban government (the U.S. version of the story is that the program ran out of money).

The whole sordid saga is one more embarrassing fool's errand in our nation's Keystone Cops effort to covertly sabotage a sovereign neighbor. The irony of it all is that when the news broke of the prisoner release, René was broadcasting it all over his real Twitter account. At the time, only 5 percent of his fellow citizens could access his play-by-play, so the word spread from these tweeters by way of texting and word of mouth. The low percentage of internet users is sure to rise dramatically and quickly. Already, representatives from both Twitter and Google have visited the island and met with government officials to plan the expansion, without the aid of USAID or any other spy agencies.

Rut Vivian Coba Cervantes with her sketch pad

The ZunZuneo project causes me to think back on an afternoon in La Vallita (where I am fairly sure no one was among the forty thousand subscribers to the social media site). Rut Vivian arrived home from school sometime between 3:00 and 4:00, and as soon as she got in the door she beckoned me to follow her out into the yard. ¡*Veo!* she cried out gleefully, pointing at a flowering bush in the corner of the yard. *What is it?* I asked. *Veo, ¡el zunzun!* We spent about a half hour watching the hummingbird flit from one flower to another in the yard. I went inside and got my camera, and kept trying to snap its photo, but the zunzun seemed to know when the shutter was going to click, and darted away just in time to avoid being captured.

Rut had a better idea. She got a piece of paper and some drawing pencils, and went to work. She has great artistic talent. We have a growing collection of her drawings, many of them portraits of us or her family or her friends. She does not draw many selfies. I wonder how long it will take for the Facebook phenomenon to reach her corner of the world. I know I should not begrudge any community getting access to the technology that I use every day, but there is something in me that does hope for long delays in the broadband access. It is the part of me that romanticizes life in the countryside, where children still spend time outside gazing in wonder at hummingbirds. It is the part of me that hopes Rut Vivian really will be *la última*, the last one to abandon sketch pads for the crowds gathered outside some hotspot, sending selfies for the scrolling world to see.

Chapter Eighteen

5:00 P.M. – Sweets

I just had to look.
–Lennon/McCartney

We're going to celebrate big-time this new year... I want to hug the five and all their families for this important achievement, for this victory of our Revolution, of our peoples, because it is not only a victory for our people but for the people of the United States in their spirit of solidarity that has also been part of this harvest.
–Mariela Castro Espín, December 17, 2014

Todo está mamey.
(Everything's peachy. Literally: Everything is *mamey*, another sweet fruit)
–Cuban expression

I wound up buying the last three international calling cards Etecsa had available. At ten CUCs a pop, with each call being over one CUC a minute, I figured thirty minutes would be sufficient for brief check-ins over the next few days until we could get our flight. After making the purchase, I headed back toward campus, where in an hour we would be feasting with the seminary community at their annual Christmas banquet. As I walked back along Milanes Street, I could not help peeping in people's windows to catch some of *Mesa Redonda* (*The Roundtable,* Cuba's daily version of *Meet the Press*) on Canal Educativo 2. While all Cuban households have windows open, enabling passersby to view what is happening inside, it is generally considered bad manners to catch more than a quick passing peek. Slowing down or stopping to steal some TV time is definitely outside the bounds of proper etiquette, unless there is a baseball game in progress and you need to see how the hometown Cocodrilos are faring.

I confess I was not minding my manners that afternoon as I paused every few houses to watch the "man on the street" interviews being conducted. I just had to look. I wanted to see how the Cuban populace was reacting to Raúl's big announcement. What I saw and heard was all positive. The segment included an impromptu interview with a very excited Mariela

Castro, who also had trouble curbing her enthusiasm at the diplomatic achievement her father had realized.

Mesa Redonda was interesting, but I realized that even though my curiosity was satisfied, something else was calling my attention. My sweet tooth had not been satiated all day. The morning rehearsal had caused me to miss my midmorning walk down the street, where I always had several options for satiating the craving for sweetness: a mere two pesos (ten cents) would get me either the chocolate bonbons next door, a block of peanut butter fudge a couple of doors down, or a cone of churros on the corner. Churros are like little pieces of freshly fried funnel cake, placed in a little paper cone and sprinkled with sugar. I always admired the guy on the corner who endured the Cuban sun while standing over the hot grease all day churning out the churros.

I thought about Kim's dad as I began reflecting on what treat I would indulge in that day. If there was something he loved more than coffee, it was the sweets that accompanied it. He and I shared a weakness for the dulces. Kim and I had long wished he could have made the trip to sample the many sugar delivery devices the islanders had engineered.

You did not, however, have to settle for the baked and fried goods of restaurants and particulares to feel sweetness on the palate. Cuba has one of the richest varieties of sweet tropical fruits on the planet. *Mamey* ranks up there as one of the most delectable. You open up this member of the apricot family when it is good and ripe, and you can take a spoon and eat it as if you were eating a bowl of pudding. It makes a fantastic shake. Same with the *chirimoya*, and the *anón*. The *fruta bomba* (aka *papaya*, which you do not say in western Cuba because of its vulgar connotation there) is standard fare when in season, often made into marmalade to enjoy with a slice of white cheese (same with the *guayaba*). The seminary students made fun of me for using my marmalade as a condiment for the mystery meat. When you do not have ketchup (pronounced *k'choop* in Cuban Spanish), you have to improvise.

I loved the pineapple (nothing like what passes for pineapple in our produce sections) and the many varieties of banana, also nothing like a Chiquita exported from Costa Rica. Mangos were Kim's favorite. When our friendly street vendor, Omar, informed us we were at the end of mango season, Kim got up early the following Sunday morning to make the two mile walk to the Cocodrilos baseball stadium parking lot, where the weekly tailgate market was held. She stood in line for quite a while to get the last of the mangos, which we cut up and froze in anticipation of a Christmas morning treat.

Even with all these choices of fresh fruits, the flavor of which we had never come close to finding in a U.S. supermarket, the cash crop of

Cuban cultivation is sugar cane. From the beginning of colonization with the Spanish, and on through U.S. and then Soviet control, Cuba's fertile land has been "enslaved to the production of sugar" to use Paco Rodés' description. Which means the economy has been captive to the ups and downs of a single source commodity.

Dagmar from Piedrecitas enjoying some sugar cane

For me, one of the puzzles of the Cuban Revolution was its embrace of this mono-crop economy. Presumably, Fidel and company were basing their revolutionary government on the best and most progressive scientific thinking the world had to offer as they engineered their health and education systems. By the end of the 1950s, the best science should have been telling them that reliance on sugar was a bad deal. Mono-crops were dangerous to both soil and economic stability (lessons learned from the Irish potato famine), and this particular mono-crop was not good for the health of the people (diabetes is a huge problem in Cuba). Nevertheless, the revolutionary leaders fully embraced raising cane, especially when the Soviets came in to provide tractors and the oil to run them.

In the late 1960s, all roads led to the sugar cane fields when Fidel Castro called for a *gran cosecha*, a great harvest, setting ten million tons as the goal in an effort to reverse an economic decline. All hands were on deck, with people from all sectors—health, education, manufacturing, engineering—taking a break from their day jobs and heading to the fields to cut cane. I should say that *almost* all hands were called on deck. People affiliated with the Church were not invited. That did not stop young pastor Paco Rodés from leaving his post and joining the effort. The Young Communist leaders heading up the effort in the fields where he arrived did not meet him with open arms. *What are YOU doing here?* They asked incredulously. *I love my country just like you,* he said, *and I can cut cane like anybody else.*

Paco had already suffered imprisonment for "holding illegal meetings," as he served a church in a rural village that was not licensed to be a church. Most pastors in similar situations fled the country. Paco and others refused to leave. He was committed to proving to the government that the Church was not counterrevolutionary, that the values of the gospel were in line with the social justice aims of the revolution, bringing good news to the poor, healing to the infirm, and release to the captives.

Paco had something else to teach the student leaders there as they cut cane together. One afternoon he was listening to a radio when the news came that Martin Luther King had been assassinated. The young pastor started weeping. When the Communist leaders asked him what was wrong, and he told them, they scoffed, *Why are you grieving over the death of some bourgeois gringo?* He began teaching them who King was, that there had been a true prophetic voice for justice there in the land of their enemy, and that they could all learn much from this prophet.

Most all Cubans of a certain age have their own *gran cosecha* stories. Some will chuckle that while the great harvest was not successful (they fell short of the goal by almost two million tons), it did give them something of great value: Los Van Van, the country's long-running pop music dance band, still going strong. Juan Formell, the late bassist and founding leader of the band, once explained that part of the propaganda of the great harvest was a motivational phrase heard a thousand times, from morning to night, on the radio, television, on billboards: *de que van, ¡van!* A literal translation does not make sense, but it generally means something like *they (the tons of sugar) are going, they keep going!*

When Formell and friends were first forming their band and were looking for a name, he wanted something catchy, like *Bam! Bam!* (while the Flintstones are shown on Cuban TV, I doubt the Rubble boy was Formell's influence). It suddenly dawned on the band leader to suggest these earworm words from the slogan, and thus was born Los Van Van. A crop failure contributed to the most popular band in the country's history.

In recent years, with the commodity prices falling dramatically, the government has closed down roughly two-thirds of the sugar plants. You would not know it by driving through the countryside, though, passing by miles and miles of cane swaying in the breeze. Neither would you know it by the diet. I doubt that desserts have been cut by two-thirds.

On a trip east, we visited a small, family-run sugar cooperative, where we chewed on some cane stalks and sampled many of the delivery devices for the sweet juice being pressed out from the stalks fed through a hand-turned mill. The first offering is the juice itself, called *guarapo*, enjoyed straight or with a shot of the fermented juice (home distilled, not Havana Club, which we might someday see in our ABC stores if the embargo ever lifts). While you can argue that Cuba's economic woes are self-induced (the flaws of socialism), the government is probably close to accurate in claims that the embargo has cost them hundreds of millions of dollars if not billions in rum revenue alone. I do suspect that a well-mixed Cuba Libre would be a popular item for U.S. bartenders to mix.

Rut Vivian Coba Cervantes with some cake

Beyond guarapo and rum and coke, the processed sugar makes its way into a myriad of dessert offerings. There is the standard cake (pronounced *kay*), with tons of icing (called meringue), and there is the stand-alone meringue puff, which is like a homemade marshmallow. There are buñuelos, a Cuban donut or beignet similar to the churros but with some starchy vegetables mixed in the batter and served with guarapo syrup. To beat the heat, they have *helado* (ice cream) of many flavors served up by street vendors in cones (with the local variety not only much cheaper but far superior to the Nestles sold in the CUC stores). I learned late in our trip that I had gotten a great reputation in the neighborhood when people saw me standing in the long line on Calle Medio with my three pesos in hand, instead of going into the *shopping* for a dollar tub of Nestles or a fifty-cent Sandy.

Experience taught us to be careful how much we rave about any particular dessert offered up at the end of a home-cooked meal. The Cubans will take such praise to mean that they should serve that exact dessert every time you visit. Which is not a bad thing, as we thoroughly enjoy the fare, but it made us feel bad that they would go to so much trouble for us. María makes incredible flan, and since we told her so on our first dinner in her home, she makes it for us every time. Same with Mabel and buñuelos. Same with Amaury in La Vallita with cremita de leche, except he does not whip up this sweetest of all desserts. He rides his bike several miles to the person he considers the best confectioner of this particular treat. Cremita de leche has a fudge-like consistency, but basically tastes like butter and sugar. When I got back home I looked up the recipe online, but Google only gave me the shortcut version: stick a can of sweetened condensed milk in the pressure cooker. Not the same.

The only way to put more sweetness in your mouth is to spoon the sugar in directly, which I saw once at the seminary merienda, when Victor was serving up café and little 5-year-old Victor Junior was sneaking some out of the sugar bowl behind his father. I have not seen the stats on diabetes in Cuba, but I suspect it must be higher than average, given the ready availability of all things glucose. Sila has had a battle on her hands for years, managing her insulin and sugar, reading the levels several times a day. It is not easy negotiating meals for diabetics there, given the dangers associated not only with the dessert fare, but with the staples of rice and beans.

I was nearing the seminary and I still had not decided which of the doors of the family sweet shops to approach, whether to go for the bonbon or the peanut butter fudge, when a voice in the distance made my decision for me. It was Jorge, the baker of pies who sold his wares out of a box on the front of his bicycle every afternoon. In another life, if Jorge was not a baker, I imagine he could make it in the world of opera. All the street vendors have clear, ringing voices, but his solid tenor trumpeting out *pie! pie de guayaba!, pie de coco!* has an operatic aria quality to it unmatched by any of his peers who added to the street chorus with their calls for bread or garlic or cheese.

I followed the sound of this Pavarotti plea for pie customers, and when I caught up with him gave my standard greeting: *that's the most beautiful song in the city!* He responded with the sweet smile that matched his wares, and asked me how the world was treating me. *Todo está mamey*, I said. *Well, actually, it's not*, I amended, filling him in on the family news and asking him to remember Kim's dad in his prayers. He promised to do so, and then reached in to find a guava pie, which I always requested, never having acquired a taste for coconut. I handed him the one CUC coin, and we parted ways. As I started up the last hill to the seminary, I took my one bite, all that I needed to satisfy my sweet tooth's urge, and put the rest in my *jabita*, my shopping bag, to share with students the next day, in celebration of the day's big news. It was not all that much, but in the hopes of doing my part to foster the spirit of solidarity, I wanted to share some of my day's *cosecha*, the harvest of my walk to town. I knew they would appreciate the gesture.

Chapter Nineteen

6:00 P.M. – Imagination

Imagine there's no countries.
–John Lennon

There's a complicated history between the United States and Cuba.
–President Obama, December 17, 2014

Pues, imagínate.
(Well, imagine that.)
–Cuban expression

I arrived back at our seminary apartment with a half hour to spare before the banquet, just enough time for the ritually observed afternoon bath. Well, they do not really take baths in Cuba, unless it's a sponge bath over a basin. Generally, it is a shower. Unlike many facets of Cuban culture that are differently observed in the East and West, in the city and country, this tradition holds true across the board, no matter the context. While in U.S. culture we have the division between those who have their bath or shower first thing in the morning versus just before bed, the Cubans opt for the late afternoon. Paco Rodés describes this as one of the deliberate delights of the Cuban culture, delineating the border between work time and leisure time. Being the theologian he is, Paco describes it as something of a baptism, a daily cleansing that prepares one for the freedom and new life that wait after the drudgery of a day's work.

The experience of a Cuban shower is one thing that we have observed evolving over the two decades we have been traveling there. In the 1990s, there was one faucet, and one temperature: cold (or tepid, depending on the weather). Eventually some of the hotels and bed and breakfasts invested in hot water heaters, which were small systems hooked into the shower head, with wires exposed. Not something to inspire confidence, and more than one visitor I know had a bit of a shock in trying to turn the heater on or off. As I was never hoping for an instant curly perm, I always opted for the cold or tepid experience. The systems have improved over the years, although some are still in view inside the shower stall.

For the country folks, like Sila and family and their neighbors in La Vallita, the shower stall has a drain but no spigot. The water is pumped into a bucket from the neighbor's well, and carried into the bathroom. A pint-size dipper functions as a self-serve shower head. Wanting to give their *yuma* guests a bit of the comforts of home, Cheo began heating a pot of water to pour into the shower bucket for us. I think I finally convinced him that I preferred the colder shower. It was a refreshing break from the Cuban heat. I even read in Medical Daily that cold showers are better for you in several aspects (countering depression, improving immunity and circulation, reducing muscle soreness, etc), more evidence that the comforts of wealth are not all that beneficial to health. That may account for my staying in such good health during the year in Cuba. In the hotter months I was taking three or four cold (as cold as I could get it) showers a day.

At any rate, I shaved and took my one shower that Wednesday afternoon, and got out the suit and tie I had packed for special occasions. The last time I had taken advantage of an opportunity to deck out in my Sunday best was in November, when the seminary students invited us to join them for their annual free day excursion, a pre-exam beat-the-stress event. We boarded a Pastors for Peace bus and headed to Havana for an evening at the ballet, Swan Lake at the Karl Marx Theater. Before heading to the theater we stopped off at the Presbyterian church in Luyano. The church has dormitories and we were going to spend the night there after the ballet. The stop-off, I learned, was for everyone to have their afternoon shower and get spiffied up. I laughed at all the guys in the men's dorm who had packed irons and were busy pressing their slacks and *guayaberas* (the Cuban four-pocket dress shirt).

The ballet was tremendous. Cuba is world-renowned for its fine arts, and this gave me pause once again to observe the contradictions of Cuban life. Here was an auditorium filled with people making far less than our minimum wage, who were nonetheless far more attuned to the intricacies and subtleties of Tchaikovsky's ballet than the vast majority of their wealthier neighbors to the North. I was reminded of a time in La Vallita, when I sat and watched Russian opera on TV with Cheo. No doubt this farmer was far more attuned to the intricacies and subtleties of Prokofiev than I could ever hope to be. Cubans may be country, but bumpkins they are not.

It was fun to arrive at the cafeteria for the banquet and see the contradictions at work again, "lower class" people who are as "classy" as they come. The entire seminary community was decked out, elegant dresses and finely coiffed hair for the women, freshly pressed *guayaberas* and slacks for the men. The Dean, Francisco Marrero, summoned me to the front, where a mic was set up, as I was part of the pre-banquet offering. He had requested that I lead the community in singing John Lennon's *Imagine* in celebration of the new day of diplomacy for our two countries.

When I first met Marrero, I was intimidated, not sure of my Spanish, not sure that my course would contribute anything useful for their curriculum. The ice broke, though, when the Dean returned from a trip to Germany, where he had participated in an international conference of biblical scholars (he teaches Hebrew scripture), and he was excited to have found a set of DVDs on the Beatles' early years, including their time in Germany.

As I worked with Carlos, the a.v. guy, on a sound check of the mic, and as he fiddled with his computer to try to re-establish a connection with the projector for lyrics to show up on screen, I thought back to how many people had requested this same song in our various travels across the island. It was definitely a favorite, perhaps only second to the Eagles' *Hotel California*, which is wildly popular there for reasons I never understood. *Imagine* I can understand. I had fun using the song in Kim's English class. Each week, we dedicated the last fifteen or twenty minutes of class to a Beatles song, using the lyrics to practice pronunciation, learn vocabulary, and introduce idioms. At the end of the semester the students and I offered a Beatles sing-along concert for the seminary community.

When it was the week to use *Imagine* for vocab and pronunciation, I added another feature to the lesson plan: a class discussion over the merits of John Lennon's dream. We took each aspect–a world with no heaven, no countries, with no religion, with no possessions–and I became devil's advocate, saying that his dream sounded terrible to me. I knew they all loved the song, so I was baiting them to get reactions, but the requirement was for their reactions to be in English.

Alicita took the bait and became spokesperson for her classmates, who all disagreed with my critique. *What do you mean, no countries?* I asked. *I appreciate the diversity of all the world's countries, France and Finland, Japan and Jamaica, Canada and Cuba. Without countries, we'd lose this diversity, wouldn't we?* Alicita countered that we could have the same if not more diversity, without countries. *Just look at the diversity within the US, or within China,* she argued. *You don't need countries and borders to have diversity.* We went from verse to verse, back and forth, and it was quite useful, not only for her (and others who piped in) to practice speaking and thinking in the language, but it was a clear revelation to me of the utopian spirit still alive, if for the most part dormant, among Cuban young people. They long for peace, for the world to live as one.

When we sang the song together that evening at the banquet there was great enthusiasm, as if everyone in the room was acknowledging that the dream had traveled a bit farther along the road to fulfillment, with our countries now trading in their fighting words for conciliatory speech. The seminary's rector, Reinerio Arce, followed the song with his own utopian message of peace in his annual Advent address. Among his words were the following:

> *Christmas, in addition to being a special time of celebration, for the gesture of love and solidarity of God with humanity and creation, is moreover a time of family celebration. The family comes together to enjoy those connections of love that unify us. Today the Cuban people are full of rejoicing because five of our families are enjoying the union together. A hug of joy and solidarity to Gerardo, René, Antonio, Fernando, and Ramón, and their families.*
>
> *It has been, I am sure, the loving and reconciling action of God who has acted in hundreds of hearts, that we have, in one way or another, worked inside and outside of Cuba to make real the living moments coming out of December 17, when our President Raúl Castro and the President of the United States Barack Obama announced the liberation of the prisoners and the re-establishment of diplomatic relations between both governments. The Cuban family is happy because these families are finally reunified. The Christian family gives thanks to God for this.*
>
> *In this very special occasion in which we celebrate the birth of the child of Bethlehem, the Prince of Peace, we see that important steps have been taken toward peace and reconciliation. For this, with immense joy that Christmas produces in us, we celebrate peace. Peace that God gives us through his Son. And we join together to sing with the Angels to the shepherds of Bethlehem: "Glory to God in the Highest and on earth Peace..."*

Reinerio would know that such peace does not come easy. Even a first step toward peace, like that of the announced renewal of diplomacy, had required long and difficult work. Reinerio grew up watching his father, Sergio, a theologian who had also served as rector of the seminary, working tirelessly to build bridges of understanding between the church and the government, and between Christians of our two countries. In the complicated history of Cuba, the hardest work of peace will be that which needs to be forged between the Cubans who stayed and the refugees who fled the revolutionary society, seeking asylum in other lands. For these exiles, works of reconciliation like that of Sergio Arce or President Obama generally bring more disdain than gratitude, as they harshly criticize anyone seeking to make peace with the Castro government.

Kenny Rivera Dellundé

I came somewhat face to face (on Facebook) with this kind of disdain only a few days ago. The provocation came when I posted a photo of one our students, Kenny, flashing a peace sign and sporting a T-shirt featuring a drawing of John Lennon a la Che Guevara, red-starred beret and all. I had used the photo in a slideshow during our end-of-semester Beatles concert at the seminary. I tagged Kenny in the post, which meant his Facebook friends could see it and could respond. One of these, an exile from Matanzas now living in the UK, posted this comment (translated): *An allegory of two international idiots! Che, a complete s.o.b. Above all a murderer. The other an addict, brilliant in his poetry, who wanted to be a hippie and live in the big apple, New York. At any rate this second was a half foolish rocker and didn't do any damage to anybody, but the first was a serial murderer! So Kenny, I don't know what to say to you brother, but I would not wear that shirt.*

I gave a short reply asking him to calm down a bit, that it was just a T-shirt mashing up a couple of cultural icons. Which provoked more exilic vitriol: *Ernesto Guevara de la Serna a cultural icon? Or assassin and coward. I don't see any culture in Che Guevara. The other was a good composer. (I am a fan of the Beatles.)* I responded that I appreciated his having an opinion, but that not everyone in Cuba shares his perspective (on Che). There are folks there, people of faith, who do appreciate the work Che did in the Revolution, who continue to be loyal to the Revolution's goals. To which I got another lengthy response about how any Cuban who looks kindly on Che and the Revolution is suffering from Stockholm Syndrome, that the Cuban government is fascist to the core. He likened Cuba's leaders to Hitler and Mussolini, and the country to one big concentration camp. He closed the exchange with *Todo eso lo digo con respeto* (I say all this with respect).

I asked a couple of my Cuban friends about the exchange, and they seemed amused. This is the kind of incendiary language the nationals have heard from exiles for fifty years. One of my students messaged me saying the Cubans have phrases for what I had done (provoking a fiery argument). He laughed (the *je je je* Facebook laugh) and said I was guilty of *encender el caldo* (firing up the soup) or *hecharle leña al fuego* (throwing kindling on the fire). To which I responded, *¡Pues, imagínate!* Imagine that!

Chapter Twenty

7:00 P.M. – A Time for Peace

Looking up I noticed I was late.
–Lennon/McCartney

This is a new chapter for the country.
– Representative Chris Van Hollen,
December 17, 2014, MSNBC interview

lista que lista
(ready, so ready)
–Cuban expression

We thoroughly enjoyed feasting at the banquet, and delighted in the sense of community as everyone pitched in, helping to get the platters of food served onto the tables for the family-style meal. The standard *arroz congrís* (rice and black beans mixed) was surrounded by pulled pork and roasted chicken, yucca with mojito, green beans, fruit salad, and a green salad. For an extra treat, we even had bread sticks and canned soft drinks (rarely seen on the seminary tables). Topping if all off was a saucer of ca' and ice cream.

    We did not get to hang around as was our custom, to help Mamita and Walquidea wash dishes. We were feeling pressed for time to get to the theater. A Pastors for Peace bus was on hand for the seminary community, but it would be arriving at the theater just in time for the event, and we were supposed to be there an hour ahead of time. So we said our thanks and our beg your pardons to the kitchen staff, and walked out to the seminary gate to wait for our ride. We had arranged with taxi-driver Orlando to come pick us up in his *máquina*. Being the North Americans we are, we were there at the gate a couple of minutes early. *¿Lista?* I asked Kim. *Lista que lista.* Ready, good and ready. So we waited. And we waited. And waited. Nervous sweat started to pop out.

    We had many occasions like this, when we had to remind ourselves that we were on Cuban time, so relax. Let go of the anxiety. All would be well. Sometimes we even had the good grace to remember what we had learned from fellow workers at the Kairos Center, that there is North

American time, there is Cuban time, and then there is Kairos time, God's time. This is the time referenced in the old spiritual, which says God may not be there when we expect, but is always right on time, as an "on-time God." We learned that waiting and letting go of the need for control are essential spiritual practices when it comes to living in Kairos time.

I am reminded of those sets of interviews I did with pairs of people sharing similar vocations in the U.S. and Cuba, and how the word *entrega*, i.e. *surrender*, kept popping up in the responses of the Cubans. There is a depth of trust required for life in Kairos history, a faith that compels you to surrender, to let go of the need to control your destiny. We learned throughout the year, including this evening at the seminary when we waited for Orlando, how much we needed to practice that art of surrender. Despite how many times we sing *I Surrender All* in U.S. churches, we cannot get around the anxious reality of a control-based culture that is deeply embedded in our psyches. A year in Cuba only served to begin the process of learning to surrender.

Orlando did not keep us waiting all that long. He showed up with his signature broad smile, opened the trunk of the old Chevy for the guitar and dulcimer to find a space between the five-gallon reserve gas cans, and away we went, dodging potholes in the ten-minute trip to Versalles. We entered the Athens Theater to find we were "right on time" to help Wanda and the youth group put the finishing touches on the programs. They were attaching small origami peace cranes to the top right corner of each bulletin, a perfect symbol for this Advent event that had as its theme *Prince of Peace*. We had been with the youth group at the seminary the day before, assembling around 350 of these cranes, made from the pages of old discarded magazines.

The Cubans are a crafty people, able to make use of whatever is available and transform it into a work of art. I think about the genius of Pancho Rodríguez, who writes and directs and acts in street theater with his troupe from the Teatro Mirón. Their costumes come from materials right out of the junk heap: hundreds of bottle caps completely cover a pair of pants for a dazzling prince, or a tea kettle is transformed into a helmet for Don Quixote. Equally creative is Danielis, a member of the little church in La Vallita, who teaches arts and crafts to children. She led a craft project when one of our church groups visited La Vallita and brought some paint and sketch pads. Danielis first had the kids go out and collect leaves of different shapes and sizes. Then she had them paint the leaves and use them as stamps to create works of abstract art on the page. These folks would be treasures at Vacation Bible School planning sessions.

We were led in our slick magazine paper origami by Reimelys, a 20-something *gallega* (Spanish descent) with sandy brown hair. She patiently demonstrated and gave us detailed instructions on how to assemble the cranes (she had to repeat the instructions many times for me, as my origami figures were not turning out very crane-like). I confess I also kept asking for help so she could practice her English with me. Reimelys, who is the communications coordinator for the Kairos Center, also serves from time to time as translator for church groups who come to visit Cuba, and I love to hear her speak English. For some odd reason, it comes out with a Russian, not Spanish, accent.

These youths were a fun and creative group to be with: Kenny is a painter, Denny is a potter, Ana María is a photographer, Kevin is studying music, while Ingrid, Jorge and Deivis are into theater. I am sure some kind of creative artistry is in the blood of the rest of the group as well. I have yet to meet an unimaginative or uninspired Cuban when it comes to the arts. Kim and I were not the only non-Cubans hoping some of this creativity would rub off: Manolo took a break from studies to join in the origami fun. He is a seminary student from New York City with family roots in the Dominican Republic. He is also the site director for the Pastors for Peace program, helping the Cuban church leaders decide where the donated buses and goods go.

In this role Manolo has another responsibility. He mentors the hundred or so U.S. students who are studying at the Medical School in Havana, a Pastors for Peace project enabling young people from poor communities to earn a debt-free doctorate in medicine in exchange for a commitment to practice back in their home settings, in some of the most challenged communities in our country. There is definitely an art and craft to that work as well. Manolo shared with us that after several years of this project, research now exists showing how well these doctors do when they return to their communities. The program gets high marks, with studies showing that graduates are well-prepared for almost all scenarios they encounter. Almost all. The returning docs have to do some on-the-job training in how to treat gunshot wounds, something unfortunately required in our emergency rooms but having little reason to be covered in Cuba's medical contexts.

Our conversation around the crafts table that afternoon skipped around many topics, occasionally coming back to the story of the origami project itself, the peace cranes. Not everyone had heard the story of Sadaku Sasaki. Between us we could collaboratively compile the essentials of the narrative: She was two years old when the atomic bomb fell on her home town of Hiroshima, and ten years later, in 1955, she was diagnosed with leukemia and given a year to live. In her nursing home she started folding the paper cranes, because she had heard the legend that whoever folded one thousand cranes would have a wish granted. Her wish was simply to live.

In one of her poems, Sadaku penned, *I will write "peace" on your wings, and you will fly all over the world*. There is some dispute over how many she folded before she died, but no matter the count, you can argue that her wish was ultimately granted. She inspired so many with her story that she indeed lives on, her spirit residing in all those who continue to fold the cranes as a prayer for peace in our war-torn world.

Origami dove backdrop at the Teatro Atenas for the Advent Celebration

Today a statue of Sadaku holding a golden crane stands in the Hiroshima Peace Park, and the family has donated some of her own cranes to bring hope to traumatized spaces like the 9-11 Memorial. At the Athens Theater in Matanzas on that December night, large replicas of the cranes were suspended from the stage ceiling, creating a backdrop for the night's participants and performers. Thanks to Reimelys and the youth group, each person in the audience would have their own peace crane to take home as a keepsake, attached to their programs.

Sadaku's story has a lot to teach about hope in the midst of tragedy and faith in the power of life over death. There have been many occasions over the past year and a half, from the time we arrived in Cuba until recent days, to call on such hope and faith. In this stretch of time there have been many kairos experiences, fullness-of-time moments, associated with loss of loved ones. While we were in Cuba we had several friends who were able to share Kim's experience of losing a parent: Tony Santana lost his father, Mabel Perera lost her father, Santiago Delgado lost his mother, and Samuel Aguilera lost his father. Since we returned a few months ago, we have learned of the death of Ernesto Bazán's father, Sila Reyna's mother, Reinerio Arce's father, and most recently Orestes Roca's father. All with broken hearts blinded by grief. All guided by faith and hope.

Our common losses remind us that a generation is passing in Cuba and in our country. Now, in this new chapter of our history, it is another generation's turn, and the door has at least opened a bit for a new set of players—Kenny and Reimelys and Denny and Ana María and Ingrid and Jorge and Rut Vivian and Karina and Nailen—to give voice to their hopes for a better world. It is their kairos time. The citation at the base of Sadaku Sasaki's statue represents what I hear from them: *This is our cry. This is our prayer. Peace on Earth.* The young people we have come to know, both from East and West, urban and rural, and now North and South, appear to us to be ready, so ready for some peace to invade their world. *Lista que lista.*

Part Five

Artists, Prophets, and Pitchers

8:00 P.M. - 12 midnight

Chapter Twenty-One

8:00 P.M. – Angels

a lucky man who made the grade...
–Lennon/McCartney

*The progress made in our exchanges proves that
it is possible to find solutions to many problems.*
–President Castro, December 17, 2014

La tercera vez es la vencida.
(Third time's the charm.)
–Cuban expression

As the Matanzas crowd began filling the theater, Kim and I took our places in the wings of the stage. As other performers and speakers made their way backstage, I was overcome with a surge of gratitude and jubilation. It had dawned on me just how fortunate, how blessed, how lucky I was, to be there, in that place, on that day, to celebrate Advent, to celebrate historic good news, with people I had come to love like family. Even my part on the program would go off without the cursed hitch that had plagued my part of the last two years' Advent celebrations. The third time really is the charm.

We would be there in the wings all evening, hanging out with Harry and Yivi, save for the time we were playing our piece on stage. As the Kairos Center's Coordinator of the Arts and Coordinator of Liturgy, respectively, Harry and Yivi were the producers and stage managers of the event, calming everyone's nerves and ensuring that they were ready when it was their time, adjusting the stage setup for each performer or speaker, and making sure the evening flowed. What a year we had enjoyed with Harry. I loved hanging around the practice room for the weekly rehearsals of Agua Viva, the musical ensemble he directed. Along with conducting the songs (many of which he had composed), he also played bass, kept a cowbell going with one foot, and sang lead. Each of these three components had a different rhythm, accompanied by yet another rhythm set by Lázaro Pomares, the percussionist.

Yivi Cruz Suárez and Harry Gerardo Castillo

As much as I worked at it, I never mastered the complex Cuban rhythms. It killed me the way Harry would anticipate the measures with his bass, playing the downbeat not on the first beat, but on the fourth beat of the previous measure. I always felt like the swan on dry land in Rilke's poem, lumbering along awkwardly through songs, as if my legs were tied. Harry is the swan in the water, moving gracefully through the currents. Add to that skill his silky smooth vibrato-laden voice and an exuberant stage presence, and you have the complete musical package. The good thing about Harry coordinating the program and stage managing was our getting to sit and cut up with him all evening. The bad thing was that we would not get to hear Agua Viva perform.

We were delighted as well to have Yivi in the wings with us, even though it meant not hearing her violin and voice in the Agua Viva ensemble. Yivi and her girlfriend Elaine had decided they were daughters to Kim and me, in an odd sort of way. Yivi and Kim have very similar personalities and outlooks on life, so Yivi decided Kim would be a second mom for her. Likewise, Elaine and I have similar personalities and outlooks, so she started calling me *Padre*. Here was the odd part: they decided that these connections of personality meant I was Yivi's *suegro* (father-in-law), and Kim was Elaine's *suegra* (mother-in-law). Suffice it to say we enjoyed our mother-daughter and father-daughter and in-law times.

Yivi was a hoot to have in the wings of the stage. To use a dated description, but one that is apt, Yivi is *cool*, one of the coolest people I have ever met, with an Arthur Fonzarelli-like aura about her (to use a dated reference). She even had a Fonzie-like greeting, reaching out for a handshake and pulling it away with a thumbs up and a yell of *¡echa!* (literally *throw down*, but loosely translated something like *hey!*).

Yivi Cruz Suárez

The theme for the night's program, Prince of Peace, also found emphasis in the text from the Christmas story where the angels announce peace on earth, good will to all. Members of the local Soldiers of the Cross church (an indigenous Cuban denomination not to be confused with the Salvation Army) read the text, dressed in their customary white. Wanda had given us free rein on our musical selection this year, and because of the angelic message of peace, we chose a medley of angel carols: *Hark the Herald*, *Angels We Have Heard on High*, and *Angels from the Realms of Glory*. I threw in a special tidbit for Orestes. As an homage to his love for rock and roll, I worked up an intro and an outro to the medley with the guitar riff from the Black Crowes' haunting song, *She Talks to Angels*. I suspected that Orestes would be the only one to catch the leitmotif, and it is a pretty sure bet that I was right.

As I looked around at all the various people we would share the stage with, it occurred to me that Kim and I were surrounded by angels. All around were messengers bringing us good tidings of peace, encouraging us to fear not, in this time when our hearts were heavy with worries about Kim's dad. We even had Leticia, an honorary member of the Kairos Center staff, there wearing her angel outfit, wings and all. The only thing missing this year was the Down's Syndrome choir that she sings with; they were an audience favorite two years prior.

Leticia Rodríguez Perez

Leticia is in her 40s, and never fails to be at the Center, where she sits in the lobby and greets people, and then has the job of ringing the bell when it is lunchtime for the staffers. She is a fan of the soaps, and sometimes picks up some bad language habits from the shows, making her lobby greeting work a little sketchy. I still have the image clearly etched into my mind from the year before, the Advent celebration in the park, when she was there in her angel costume. When I approached her to wish her a feliz navidad, she flipped me the bird. Another bad habit from TV watching, but it made for a priceless encounter in costume.

The program began with a youth theater troupe, Revelaciones, invoking the spirit of Advent with an abstract re-creation of the birth of the Christ child. Another drama team would enact mini-scenes of a contemporary search for the meaning of the story throughout the evening. The musical offerings began with a woodwind trio playing *O Come, O Come, Emmanuel.* We had gotten to know Lisbeth, the oboist of the trio, through other musical events and SOMOS gatherings. I am impressed with anyone who can make music with an oboe, and she is a consummate artist on the instrument. She is soft-spoken, when she does speak (which is not often), so it was hard for me to gauge what she was thinking or feeling at any given time.

Once, I thought I had upset Lisbeth, when I put a copy of *The Lord is My Shepherd* from Rutter's *Requiem* onto a thumb drive to give to her, along with the sheet music. It has a sublime oboe part, so I had an idea that she could play it with the Matanzas Chamber Choir someday. I could not wait for her to hear it, so one evening after a church event I had her put in the earphones and listen to it through my laptop. It is a five-minute piece, and halfway through, it looked like she had a pained expression on her face, causing me to sweat out the last couple of minutes, worrying that she hated it. My fears abated when she took the earphones out, and with watery eyes told me it was the most beautiful thing she had ever heard in her life. I still hope to hear her play it with the choir sometime.

The trio was followed by a sweet old couple, Dinarda and Héctor, who had performed their duets at the previous two events as well, the man playing traditional Cuban rhythms on guitar and singing harmony for his spouse who sang lead. With their 70-something voices a bit shaky but right on pitch, and with their obvious affection for one another, they were an audience favorite each year. They gave me and Kim something to shoot for, imagining what our music might sound like and hoping we will exude that much love after another quarter-century of marriage.

Then came an exquisite interpretive dance around the Advent wreath. The dancer was Irina González, a young Afro-Cuban woman from the Danza Espiral troupe, dressed in all white, interweaving fabric into a performance that combined contemporary and traditional sacred movements from the African faith traditions. It was mesmerizing.

Irina González, from Danza Espiral, at the Advent Celebration

Yaima, the singer I had accompanied two years prior when the guitar strap broke, was on stage following the dance, this time accompanied by piano and sax. She nailed a version of Nat King Cole's *The Christmas Song*. She had been concerned about her pronunciation of the English words, and we only had to do a little coaching on the *uh* and short *i* sounds that are virtually impossible for Spanish speakers, who do not have those vowels in their repertoire of sounds. Yaima was able to get close, improving on the *chestnoots* roasting and Jackfrost *neeping* that most naturally comes out.

Next came a jazz saxophone quartet who did a cool cover of *We Three Kings* (*cool* in the technical jazz sense, not the dated term). Their version reminded me of the scene in *Scrooged* when Bill Murray disses a street musician playing the same carol in similar cool-jazz style. When the credits rolled I learned that the street trumpeter was played by none other than the inventor of cool himself, Miles Davis. The sax quartet was a hard act to follow, but next up was our angel medley, and we did not embarrass ourselves. Various other soloists and choral groups presented throughout the evening, offering us their interpretations of those tidings of comfort and joy. We sat there in the wings and soaked in all this music, played and sung by angels.

I am writing this chapter after viewing a DVD with my nephew David of one of his favorite movies, *Inside Out*. I had not seen it. It features the animated characters of Joy and Sadness, and the movie's message is the necessity of allowing Sadness the opportunity to play her part, if you want Joy to emerge. That is what was happening to us that evening with Harry and Yivi, with Wanda and Orestes, with the musicians and singers. Our Cuban family did not shy away from acknowledging the sadness of the unfolding news of my father-in-law's last days. Yet, in their embrace of our sadness, they unlocked the passageway to a deeper joy.

Dianelys Ortega Horta and her dance partner Leo Peñate Navarro at the Advent Celebration

One of the most joyous portions of the evening's program for me was a traditional *criollo* dance, led by our dear friend, another "angel" whom we consider as another of our "daughters," Dianelys, and her dance partner Leo. Family dinners around Dianelys' table were among the most memorable of the year for me, not only because her mom and grandma are fabulous cooks, but because among her mom's specialties is homemade ketchup that rivals anything Heinz has bottled, and which satisfied a homesick longing I had suffered from for a long time. A tan *gallega* who maintains a dancer's body despite her mom's cooking, Dianelys knows how to use not only her body but also her long and thick mane of auburn hair to full effect in the course of her dance numbers.

Besides being a world-class dancer, Dianelys is also one of the brightest people I know. I am sure she could be anything she wanted to be: a surgeon, a lawyer, a teacher, a chef, or the lead ballerina in the national ballet. Like many bright young people with the capacity to do anything, though, she works in the tourist industry, leading activities for the clientele of a resort hotel in Varadero Beach.

Dianelys Ortega Horta, photo by unknown client of
Meliá Hotel in Varadero

We helped Dianelys practice for the language exam she had to pass to get this job. She needed to be able to explain the rules of volleyball in English. She is in charge of keeping the European and Canadian beachcombers occupied with all sorts of activities, volleyball, salsa dance lessons, shuffleboard, whatever. I reserve any judgment for this line of work (reminiscent of Julie from the *Love Boat*), for despite Dianelys' underutilized breadth of ability, I am sure that she is making more in tips than the country's brain surgeons, enabling her to bring home the bacon for her family.

Still, there is a sadness in the way that the Cuban economy has turned the pyramid of work upside down, with the least skilled jobs of the hospitality industry earning so much more than the highly skilled jobs, whether they be brain surgery or ballet, teaching or animal husbandry.

When people ask about how Cuba has changed or is changing since we have renewed diplomacy, my stock answer is that the most visible changes are likely to be limited to the tourist and resort sectors. I cannot imagine how these changes will reach La Vallita out in the middle of the island, far removed from any shuffleboard court.

That said, I do not sense that Sila or any of the folks there share my sadness in this unfair economic distribution of goodies. At least I have not heard anyone there complain about it. They are going about their business, which for us meant being every bit as much the company of angels as the folks there in Matanzas. I do not mean to exaggerate when I say that Sila really does have an angelic quality to her. She is a messenger, a bearer of God's love and grace to her community. Along with bringing good tidings to her church family, she has in recent years found herself being something of a hospice chaplain in the wider community, as families have called on her to help bring peace and assurance to loved ones on deathbeds.

Kim with a younger Rut Vivian

Rut Vivian also has been angel to us. I wrote earlier that while she loves to draw and color, she never does self-portraits. Then again, maybe she does, because she does love to draw angels. Later in the year Rut would become a true bearer of grace for Kim, when we got back from the States after the funeral, and had occasion to visit La Vallita. Kim was sharing with the family how her dad had loved the ocean, and how she had spread some sea shells on his grave. She had brought a few of these sea shells back with her and had taken them to put on the grave of Tony Santana's father, who had died a few months earlier.

Rut Vivian left the house after hearing the story, without telling us where she was going. She re-emerged a bit later, with something in her hand. *Here,* she told Kim, *I want you to have this.* It was a small rock, and Rut said, *I looked all around for the most special rock I could find, because I want you to take it and put it on your papa's grave, so he'll have some of La Vallita there.* Oh yeah, we talk to angels; they call us by our name. They sing sweetly o'er the plains of La Vallita and Matanzas, and in reply, the mountains of western N.C. are echoing their joyous strain. *Gloria, en excelsis Deo.*

Chapter Twenty-Two

9:00 P.M. – Prophetic Voices

Somebody spoke.
–Lennon/McCartney

Our Revolution is in no way against religious feelings, at least with the idea that we have about religion. A religion that fleshes human ambitions, that follows human noble ideals is in no way against us. Actually in our understanding this kind of religion fully coincides with our Revolution that only pursues the benefit of men and to fight against injustice.
   –Fidel Castro, December 17, 1959

¡Qué cosa más grande!
(What a great thing!)
–Cuban expression

Along with the music and dance portion of the Advent celebration, the program called for some spoken words. There was Father Miguel, the priest from El Carmen Catholic Church, offering the evening's message. There was poetry, and Orestes' sister-in-law Tulia, the Episcopal priest, was on tap for the benediction. Before the final good word, though, another voice, not on the scheduled program, was summoned. On a day like December 17, the community needed to hear from its beloved prophet and priest. So Wanda and her fellow event organizers called upon Paco Rodés, founder of the Kairos Center, retired pastor of the First Baptist Church, and founding director of Cuba's prison chaplaincy program, to put the day in perspective with a reflection.

This would be the third such Advent meditation Paco would offer to the community. Two years earlier had also been historic for the community, the first ecumenical Christmas celebration permitted in a public space, the Velasco Theater on the town square. The next year, it was the first time such an event was permitted outdoors in Liberty Park, and Paco again was called upon. That occasion had a kairos quality as well, as it coincided with the passing of Nelson Mandela, a faithful friend to Cuba, and Paco was able to weave in a tribute to Mandela in the context of his Advent message.

Francisco "Paco" Rodés speaking at the 2014 Advent Celebration

If Kim and I are blessed to count people like Sila and Cheo and Orestes and Wanda as brothers and sisters, and Elaine and Yivi and Dianelys as our Cuban daughters, we are equally blessed to count Paco and his spouse Lila as our Cuban parents. Kim is like Lila in many ways, with many fonts of creativity, energy, and while it may pain Kim to hear it, with the same proclivity for providing perpetual instructions when her spouse is driving the car! Similarly, I find Paco a real kindred spirit in at least a couple of key personality aspects. One, we are both the consummate absent-minded professors, with a whole catalog of stories of what my family affectionately calls "d.a." (dumb-ass) moments that occur when our heads are in the clouds.

One time in particular Lázaro Ceballo, at the end of a prison-chaplaincy training event, laughed and called me *Paquito* (little Paco). I had showered and changed for the closing session, and when it was over, I noticed that I was not getting the same hugs as usual. People were giving me what I call the pregnant woman hug. Lázaro pointed out that I had done the same thing Paco had once famously done: after brushing my teeth, I wanted to wash my hands and there was not any place to lay the toothbrush, so I put it in my shirt pocket, and then by the time I left the restroom I forgot it was there. The chaplains were a little leery of getting too close to my toothbrush.

I am connected to Paco in another way, too: a lack of self-confidence. I was surprised when I got to know this institution of a man who has made such an impact over the decades in the life of the Cuban church and community, that he is unsure of himself and his abilities. To hear stories from his six decades of ministry, you would never guess that he is plagued with self-doubt. He does not like to give eulogies, because he does not feel eloquent enough for those occasions. He did not feel he was a good pastor, because there were never many members of his church. What makes me love and admire him even more, in knowing this, is seeing the way he has faithfully plugged along, doing what needed to be done, in spite of this shortage of self-esteem.

To understand a bit about Paco and his faithfulness, it is good to hear him describe his calling to ministry. He was a teenager, being groomed to follow in his father's footsteps as a doctor. All of that changed when he attended a church service, and something happened to alter the course of his life. *I experienced this emotion,* he recalls, *this intimate experience, very strong, to surrender my life, to give my life to a sacrificial following of Jesus, because He spoke of taking up the cross. Soon I felt that I was called to preach. I began to preach in the missions of the church at age 15, 16. My father was a doctor, and dreamed that I would be a doctor. When I finished high school, he tried to convince me to become a doctor, that while being a doctor I could be a preacher too. But I felt that my surrender would not be complete if I didn't dedicate my life solely to the ministry.*

There's that word again, *surrender*. He was all in. I imagine he took it as encouraging news when as a young mission preacher he heard the Revolutionary hero, Fidel Castro, in another famous December 17 speech from the first year of his presidency, voicing support for religion, the kind of religion that Paco was involved in, one that *fleshes human ambitions and follows human noble ideals and fights against injustice.* Just three years later, this same hero made another historic speech, declaring that religion was antiquated and the new government of Cuba would be officially atheistic, starting a three-decade policy of official discrimination.

Early in that period Paco was arrested and jailed, on the charges of "holding unauthorized meetings" (these were house-church worship services in the countryside where he was pastor). The local authorities gave Paco the opportunity to leave his jail cell and return to freedom if he simply paid a small fine, which would be an acknowledgment of his guilt. He refused to pay the fine, and stayed in the cell with two other delinquents: one was in for public drunkenness and the other for stealing a pig. When they asked him what he was in for, he laughed and said, *for preaching against those things you did!*

Paco challenged the judge to a public debate over the role of religion in public life, and while publicly accepting the challenge, the judge never followed through to make it happen. Several of Paco's friends and fellow pastors came to encourage him to leave the jail; they would pay the fine for him. He stubbornly refused, unwilling to admit any wrongdoing. Finally, after some time had passed, an elderly man from the countryside came to town to visit Paco. *Pastor,* he said in a pleading voice. *The church needs you. Our community needs you. We need a pastor.* That was all it took. Paco paid the fine and returned to his parish. His *surrender* was total.

Part of that surrender also involved continuing his quest to prove to the government that the church was not counterrevolutionary, that it was an important part, an essential part, of the Cuban identity. It must have felt like he was tilting at windmills. It only took him and his fellow Don Quixote's three decades to accomplish their goal.

As the Soviet Union fell and left Cuba in the trenches of despair, Paco joined a group of around forty pastors in a meeting with Fidel Castro and some of his top officials. One of these officials suggested that as the Cuban people were suffering from despair, the church needed to do its job and offer hope. One of the pastors responded, *How can we do that when we are officially discriminated against?* The meeting went on, and at the end of it, Fidel Castro left with a commitment to correct this "error" of the Revolution. He and his officials amended the Constitution, and for the first time the church could realize those words from his 1959 speech. They could pursue the benefits of society without being plagued by prejudice.

It was in the throes of this decade of despair, the Special Period, that Paco prophetically announced the founding of the Kairos Center in 1994. It was the most unlikely of settings to proclaim that *kairos*—God's time—the fullness of time—was breaking into their lives. Now that I think about it, I realize that this is Paco's gift, the gift of the prophet who is able to tell people at their worst moment, *this is the time. This is the moment. Something incredible is breaking into our world.*

Those moments do not just happen on their own, without a catalyst. Inspiring spaces of creativity like the Kairos Center do not just pop up out of the blue. Interfaith collaborations between mainline churches and Afro-Cuban religious communities do not just randomly start up. Prison chaplaincy programs do not just emerge out of thin air. They are spoken into being by people like Paco, by those who do not think they have the eloquence to offer a eulogy, but who speak anyway, and people believe them. Those prophetic utterances prompt people to start fostering the arts of survival that it will take to endure whatever trauma they are facing.

There are many prophetic Paco stories to tell, and I am happy that he is writing his memoirs. He is putting pen to paper in the form of letters to his grandson, Gabriel, an 18-year-old who only gets to see his grandfather every year or two when one of them gets the opportunity to cross the border for a short visit.

Lila González, Sila Reyna, Paco Rodés, and Stan, photo by Judith Rodés

I hope that Paco includes in the book the time he enabled *kairos* to happen in the little forgotten village of La Vallita. Sila Reyna had just had her dream, again in the midst of the Special Period, that she would be pastor of a house church. She found the house of her dream in La Vallita, but had zero resources, no money, to make the dream a reality. That's where Paco stepped in, assuring her that she would be pastor of that house church. He took it on himself to seek out sources to provide the money for that house, to furnish it, so her family could move in and she could start her own prophetic and priestly work in that community.

I wish I had a transcript of the reflection Paco offered that night in the Athens Theater. When I asked him for it, he said he did not have anything written down. It was an impromptu meditation spoken from the heart. What I remember him doing in that reflection was paying tribute to the peacemakers who had worked so long on behalf of the Prince of Peace, who had toiled in the field in hopes of a day of reconciliation, but had not lived to see its fruition.

Among those was the late Lucius Walker, the founder of Pastors for Peace, who began making these connections with Cuba and building bridges decades ago. We do not do our work in isolation, Paco reminded us. Lucius Walker is among a great cloud of witnesses upon whose shoulders we stand. The way the media would frame the story, the historic renewal of diplomacy was due to the secret meetings of three people: Barack Obama, Raúl Castro, and Pope Francis. Without taking away from their courageous willingness to step through the door that was open for them, Paco challenged us not to forget the countless people of faith in both countries who had been pushing that door open for many, many years.

After Paco's reflection, and before Tulia's benediction, there was one more thing to do. All the participants gathered back on the stage: Kim and I joined Dianelys and her dance group, the woodwind trio, the jazz quartet, the elderly duo, the various choirs and soloists and dramatists, with Harry and Yivi also emerging from the wings, to lead the audience in singing *Noche de Paz*, night of peace, aka *Silent Night*. As we sang I felt again like a holy host of angels was gathered round us.

When we finished, and as Tulia was blessing us with her good words of benediction, out of nowhere it entered my mind that maybe the Sarah McLaughlin *Angel* song would have been a more appropriate mash-up than the Black Crowes' *She Talks to Angels*. When I considered how much joy was there on the stage, mixed in with the sadness of so much grief, the grief of separated families, of the loss of loved ones, McLaughlin's lilting voice ran through my mind: *it's easier to believe, in this sweet madness, oh, this glorious sadness that brings me to my knees... in the arms of an angel*. The glory of the sadness was its ability to lead us into the arms of angels, found there in the maddening contradictions that make up Cuba. There we rested, finding our comfort in the presence of good company. *¡Que cosa más grande!*

Chapter Twenty-Three

10:00 P.M. – Ordinary Time

Made the bus in seconds flat.
–Lennon/McCartney

*I do not expect the changes I am announcing today
to bring about a transformation of Cuban society overnight.*
–President Obama, December 17, 2014

hacer la botella
(hitch a ride, lit, *make the bottle*)
–Cuban expression

When you are in the middle of a kairos moment, experiencing the fullness of time, in the arms of angels, it seems like that is the center of the universe, with such depth of significance that everything must be revolving around it. It does not take long to be reminded of the folly of such an illusion. The opposite of kairos time is ordinary time, not full, not particularly significant. As soon as the Advent program was over, when Tulia said her *Amen,* ordinary time took over. After a bit of hugging and congratulating, people were scrambling to get to their rides home. We hugged and congratulated a bit too long, and missed the bus going back to the seminary.

Our friends Benny and María Victoria saw us standing there on the sidewalk, instruments in hand, watching the bus vanish in the distance, and came to our aid. Like most Cubans, they have great ingenuity when it comes to problem solving, having had ample experience. Benny is the leader of the church's Tercer Edad (senior citizen) program, and deals with logistical challenges on a regular basis. His spouse, María Victoria, coordinates the social service outreach program for the Kairos Center, another position that requires figuring out solutions. They said not to worry; they would get us a ride.

They found that Paco and Lila had not yet departed, and thought that would be a possibility, to hitch a ride in the old burro, the Russian Lada. I was fairly certain that this was not an option I wanted to try. Between fears of being in the car with absent-minded Paco behind the wheel, especially at night when his vision was significantly impaired, and the near certainty that the Lada did not have the power to climb the Dos de Mayo hill to the seminary, I decided that walking the two miles was preferable. We compromised to make it work: I would drive the Lada to the center of town, to the park (fairly level ground all the way), and then let Lila give her steering directions to Paco for their journey back home from there.

Driving the Lada was always stressful for me, as it was, in Paco's description, a communist car, with all the working parts requiring their regular breaks from work, no matter if it was in the middle of the highway. We made it to the park without incident, though, save the stress of negotiating the traffic around the Sauto Theater, remembering to yield to the Yutong buses that had just left the bus station in Pueblo Nuevo for the long ride back to the East. These were filled with the San Lázaro pilgrims who had been to the leper colony near Havana that day to pay tribute to their beloved saint.

Paco and Lila with their Lada

Seeing the Yutong buses made me think about the times in La Vallita when we had to catch buses to get back to Matanzas. We always had to stand by the carretera to hitch a ride from the village to the bus station in Camagüey, the capital city of the province, where we would get our westbound bus. Sila and Cheo would always stand there with us, with Cheo usually doing the hitchhiking, as people might have been leery of picking up *yumas* standing alongside the highway.

On one such occasion, Anabel and her girls, Rut Vivian and Lisy, joined us as well. We got to the little waiting area with a couple of benches after dinner that evening, needing to get to the bus station at 3:00 in the morning for a 4:00 departure. It was only an hour's ride to Camagüey, so we relaxed and enjoyed some of this very "ordinary" time chatting with the family as Cheo sought to "make the bottle" (Cuban slang for hitchhiking), waving his hand in Cuban hitchhiker mode with a couple of bills showing he would be a paying customer. It was a Sunday evening, meaning not much traffic on the highway going past La Vallita, and we waited for an hour, then two, then three. Not to worry, I had done this enough to know that waiting for a bus is part of the deal in Cuba, whether you are in La Vallita or Varadero or Matanzas. It is all the same. Plenty of wait time.

The worries did start setting in, though, around 10:00 that night, when what little traffic there had been all but disappeared, apparently for the night. Anabel finally gave up around 11:00 and took the girls home to bed. At midnight, Kim called the bus station to describe our plight, but there was nothing they could do. More waiting, until Sila finally rounded us up for some serious praying, which she is very good at.

I confess my lack of faith. I was resolved to go back to the house and catch some sleep and try again the next day. Not too long after Sila's *amen,* sure enough we saw headlights in the distance, a Yutong on its way to the station. It stopped for Cheo, who explained to the driver who it was needing the ride, and we hustled on, making it to the station with a full hour or so to spare. Cheo accompanied us, as he always did, to make sure we actually did get our bus for Matanzas. Then he turned around and made the bottle back home, to put in a day's work at the cooperative.

In Matanzas, it was a spectacular night for a walk when we got out of the Lada and bid Paco and Lila farewell for the night, and started making our way up Dos de Mayo. It was in this short stretch that the difference between kairos time and ordinary time became even clearer. Having a theater full of matanceros, around 300 or 350 of them, to experience the wonders of the Advent celebration meant that there were around 149,700 of the populace who did not experience those same wonders.

By all accounts, life was going on pretty much as usual in the neighborhood. The dominos game was still going on there on the corner. Dogs were competing for the bones and other food trash that had been thrown into the street from someone's evening meal. And the televisions were flickering from just about every window and open door. I couldn't help it. As we walked up the hill, I paused to see what was on, and was interested to find it was a baseball game, with the hometown Cocodrilos playing the Naranjas of Santa Clara.

Sidewalk dominoes in Matanzas

I should have guessed this would be on television; I could hear the air horns in the distance. One time at the Victoria de Girón (Victory of the Bay of Pigs) Stadium was enough for me. To be honest I could not make it past the seventh inning, as at least half the crowd had one of those blasted air horns and were blowing away, not at critical times in the game, but throughout. I preferred watching the Cocodrilos on TV. So as we walked up the hill, I paused at every third or fourth open window to catch a bit of the game. Left-handed relief pitcher Yoanni Yera was effectively shutting down the Orangemen for the good guys. Matanzas had held a 3-1 lead into the fifth, when starter Jonder Martínez gave up the tying runs. The Cocodrilos came back with one go-ahead run, and Yera kept it that way for a 4-3 victory.

Baseball reminded me that the world was spinning as usual, in Cuba and elsewhere. There might be earthshaking news, but the game goes on, and the vast majority of matanceros were probably more invested in the game than in all the ways the stars had lined up for this Advent day's celebrations. President Obama was right. The changes he was announcing would not bring about a transformation of Cuban society overnight. We climbed the last hill on the journey to the seminary, with street lights flashing off and on at random (no doubt communist lights, like Paco's car).

We walked through the gates and found a few of the students still up and about, enjoying the evening air. One, Tirisay, approached us and asked if we could play music for her the next morning in chapel. It was her turn to preach, and she wondered if we could play *We Three Kings*. Sure. With no time to prepare, it would have to be an ordinary version, standard 3/4 time, not nearly as cool or jazzy as Miles Davis. Then again, maybe having the wise men do an ordinary waltz to Bethlehem in the middle of all that kairos chaos would have its own appeal.

Fan blowing air horn in the Victoria de Girón ballpark in Matanzas

Chapter Twenty-Four

11:00 P.M. – Reflections

The English army had just won the war.
—Lennon/McCartney

Todos somos Americanos. (We are all Americans)
—President Obama, December 17, 2014

Bueno, bueno, le dijo la mula al freno.
(Well, well, said the mule to the brakes.)
—Cuban expression

Before heading up to the apartment, we walked back to the edge of campus, to sit and look down at the bay. We were not sitting on a dock, and I would not say we were wasting time, but we were watching the tide roll away as we reflected on what a day it had been. I wondered if the ramifications from this day would one day cause the graffiti on so many walls and billboards to change from *Siempre 26* to *Siempre 17*. The July 26 Movement may have run its course, and just as the aphorism tells us to never say *never*, perhaps the same can be said for *siempre*, never say *always*. Should such a December 17 movement arise, it may have its own 50-year cycle of forever as well.

The bay is incredibly alluring and mesmerizing at any time of day, but especially so at night, with the lights of the city joining the starlight and sliver of moonlight to make the water do a Dianelys-like dance. I sat there and pondered the significance of this Bay of Matanzas, the history of resistance flowing through its waters. The name itself derives from the first act of resistance: the word *matanzas* means *slaughters*, and the story of how the city and bay got their name goes all the way back to Columbus' landing and the subsequent exploration of the island.

The episode happened in 1511, when a group of Spanish conquistadors on one side of the bay wanted to cross to the other side. They conscripted some of the indigenous Taino Indians to carry them across in fishing canoes. When the caravan of canoes was midway across, one of the Taino gave a signal, and the canoes were capsized, sending all but one of the thirty heavily armored conquistadors to their watery grave. The lone survivor lived to tell the story.

Three centuries later, in 1843, Matanzas exemplified more of the resistant spirit, as a local sugar factory worker, an Afro-Cubana named Carlota, engineered the first and best known slave rebellion. While the rebellion was harshly and cruelly quelled, Carlota's name lived on, so much so that when Fidel Castro sent troops to Angola in that civil war, he named the effort Operation Carlota. In the beginning years of the Castro regime, the most famous of the Cuban resistance efforts against North American interference emerged out of Matanzas Province, as Castro's forces fought and defeated the expatriate counterrevolutionaries sponsored by the U.S. at the nearby Bay of Pigs, aka Playa Girón.

Such solid determination, such a fierce spirit of resistance emanated from this province, this city, this bay. There is a two-person Cuban expression that fits this spirit. One person might fill a pause in a conversation with a *bueno, bueno* and the conversation partner will make a rhyme, *le dijo la mula al freno*. Sort of like when someone says *well* and hears the response *that's a deep subject*. In the Cuban phrase, *well, well*, provokes the response, *said the mule to the brakes*. The first speaker might then add, *y siguió caminando* (and kept on walking). It has to do with trying to force a Cuban to do something they do not want to do. There is a headstrong willfulness about them. They are as stubborn as the proverbial mule. wondered if this fierce resistance could go on forever. Would they be able to put the brakes on whatever forces were being unleashed by the opening of relations with the U.S.?

The question caused me to chuckle as I remembered a church group that came to visit the seminary, who met one afternoon with a group of seminarians. Like too many U.S. visitors, they had been there less than a week and had figured Cuba out. They were eager to give advice to the students. One, a university professor, proceeded to lecture the students on the impending dangers of U.S. intervention, admonishing them to beware and prepare for the coming tsunami of business and political interests swelling and threatening to wash over the island.

As the professor paused his lecture to ask if the students understood what he was trying to say, one seminarian politely explained to him that they had been aware of his warning since they were in diapers. They were all well-schooled in the threatening and voracious appetite of the monster to the North. It has been drummed into their heads virtually every day of their lives. A bit of the wind came out of the sails of the long-winded professor, who thought he was cluing them in on a new revelation.

If we learned anything from our year there, it was how little we knew. Like Plato, we could say *I know that I know nothing*, and be close to the truth. The cultural and linguistic distances are vast, and misunderstandings are much more likely than genuine understandings. May that serve as a bit of a caveat to all readers of this diary. It is bound to be filled with many errors. The book is simply one observation of one thin slice of Cuban culture and life, and hopefully my Cuban friends will be gracious as they offer corrections to all the mistakes found here.

Yet and still, *seguiremos*. Like the proverbial mule, stubborn Cubans of all stripes in contexts as diverse as Centro Kairós in Matanzas and the Ríos de Agua Viva church in La Vallita keep on keeping on, in spite of all the forces that might divert their path. The determined spirit of the people I connected with finds voice in the simple verb that shows up in many of their songs: *seguiremos*. We keep on. *Andaremos por el mundo con fe y esperanza viva... seguiremos cantando y luchando por la vida.* "We will walk through the world with faith and living hope. We will keep on singing and struggling for life."

The Cuban people have kept on through many struggles, withstanding attempts at sabotage and subversion such as the Bay of Pigs, and including our country's many Keystone Cops efforts at espionage, from the CIA's cigar bombs to USAID's *fracasos* in the worlds of tweeting and hip-hop music. I did wonder, though, if even this well-proven resistance would be strong enough to withstand Facebook's allure. Could it be that animated emoticons and selfies and silly cat videos will succeed where the CIA has failed?

All that is yet to be seen. What could be seen that night, from my perch at the edge of the seminary campus, were the lights flickering over water. We often realized when we sat there with that view that we were looking toward home. Matanzas, situated on the northernmost tip of Cuba, is the famed ninety-mile point from the Florida Keys. Beyond those ninety miles, another eight hundred miles was our home, our North Carolina home.

It dawned on me that we would be home for Christmas. René González had included in his tweets that day something voiced by many people, by Reinerio and Paco and others: *todos estaremos juntos en navidad*. All will be together for Christmas. An interesting sentiment from the government spy, given how only a few short years back *navidad* had been virtually outlawed. Kim and I would also experience a Christmas family reunion.

Our return to be reunited with our family would be bittersweet, for sure, with Kim's dad passing away early in the morning on Christmas Eve. We were grateful to have been there to help usher him through that passage, sitting by his bedside, playing his favorite Christmas carols. *In the Bleak Midwinter* took on a deeper meaning, especially given the weather we came back to, snowy and bitter cold. *Frosty wind made moan, earth stood hard as iron.* One of the verses reaffirmed the theme of the Advent and Christmas season: *Angels and archangels may have gathered there.* Some days later we would experience that same quality of being carried by angels we had experienced in Cuba, as lifelong friends and family came to the funeral and expressed so much love and gratitude for a life well-lived.

When we got back to the seminary after the funeral, another angel greeted Kim, this one with four legs. She had said her goodbyes to Blanquito, the goat, before leaving, being sure that he would wind up on someone's table for the *navidad* or *fin de año* feasting. When our taxi driver drove through the gate, though, and as we opened the doors and stepped out of the *máquina*, our first greeting was a loud and enthusiastic *baaahhhh*. Blanquito had survived the feasts, proving there is more than one kind of resistance at work in Matanzas.

Of course we could not have known any of that as we sat there that night of December 17, looking at the bay, gazing northward. We were sleepy. We thought about those poor pilgrims on the Yutong bus who were headed east, on their way back to La Vallita or Holguín or Bayamo, trying to sleep in the most uncomfortable of seats. Going home.

Easter sunrise over the Bay of Matanzas, 2015

As the sleepiness prompted me to finally stand and begin walking back to our apartment, I wondered what I might dream that night. I thought about Martí's dream of unifying all the countries of Latin and North America into one America. Note that here in the book I tried never to refer to our country as America. That is something I did learn over the course of our year. While we are the United States of America, we do not have the monopoly on the name *America*. Maybe there was hope, though, that we were just a tiny step closer to realizing Marti's dream. As the popular Cuban praise song says, *Pues, en este mundo paz y amor tendremos. Unidos, siempre unidos.* Well, in this world we will have peace and love. United, always united.

My last thoughts before hitting the bed were of the more recent dream voiced by Richard Blanco, the U.S. poet with Cuban parentage, who recited these lines at President Obama's second inauguration (I had used the poem in the course I taught):

> *One sun rose on us today, kindled over our shores*
> . . .
> *One light, waking up rooftops, under each one, a story*
> *told by our silent gestures moving behind windows.*
> . . .
> *. . .always*
> *one moon like a silent drum tapping on every rooftop*
> . . .
> *Hope—a new constellation waiting*
> *for us to map it, waiting for us to name it—together.*

Epilogue

having read the book...
–Lennon/McCartney

We will continue talking about these important issues at a later date.
–President Raúl Castro, December 17, 2014

Me cae bien.
(It sets well with me, literally *It falls me well.*)
–Cuban expression

I returned to Cuba for a short visit a few months after our homecoming. I was accompanying a church group that was exploring the possibility of a partnership, and we were able to visit one church in the Santa Clara province that I had not previously visited. I had met the pastor, but did not know her or her family well. When we arrived, we greeted her and her spouse, and their two sons, one 9 and the other 11. The older boy lit up and whispered something to his mother. He recognized me–I was the tree that had fallen!

The previous February Kim and I had attended the Fraternity of Baptists annual assembly. One of our seminary students, Margot, was in charge of kids programming for the weekend meeting, and asked us to help. The Fraternity's yearlong theme, and the theme for this meeting, was "Affirming Life from Our Roots." All of the programming had something to do with the metaphor of the Church as a tree. We enacted a drama with the children, in which I was an old tree that eventually fell to the earth, but out of the soil around me many small trees emerged from the acorns my tree had produced. Cycle of life, or resurrection. At any rate, I received rave reviews for my acting job, which involved little more than some swaying followed by a sudden fall, but I hammed it up in dramatic fashion. It had made an impression on this young boy, who assured me that I had done a very good job falling.

I had fallen in Cuba, all right, in more ways than one. As I read back over my journal, and look at the photos, and feel the aching and longing in my heart and soul and gut, I realize I had fallen in love with the Cuban people. Head over heels. Somehow this frustrating and challenging environment had forged a people of such intense and incredible character, it seems impossible to me that one could not fall for them, given adequate time to get to know them.

Leaving these loved ones and returning home, especially returning for the funeral of father-in-law Ed Christman, reminded me of something else equally important, and that is my head-over-heels love for my U.S. family. As frustrating and challenging as our culture is, as individualistic and materialistic and trivial as it has come to be, Ed and the people who came to honor him reminded me that there are people of great determination and resistance in our land, too, who live with the same kind of compassion, openheartedness, and sense of community as does our Cuban family, despite all the pressures to the contrary.

Some weeks after the locust tree fell over my driveway, I had some tree specialists come to fell a few other trees that were perilously close to our house, whose canopies had spread over our roof. I asked the owner of this tree company, a man named Christian, if he would take a look at the big locust lying on the ground in the woods, and estimate its age. He examined it and said his best guess would be between fifty and sixty years old. Hmmm. Maybe this locust originally sprang from the soil around 1959, about the time a Revolution was springing from the island soil of Cuba. I do not mean to use the similarity to make any prediction about the fall of an empire or a regime change. But if changes do come (and that is one of the certainties of life, change), whatever it is that falls, I hope that it falls well. *Caer bien*. Like my tree in the children's play.

Locust trees tend to stay upright long after they die. They are stubborn. Eventually, though, their reaching for sunlight converts to a longing for the dark, where they can be reborn. Like the locusts, I figure it will take a long time for some things that have grown out of our two countries' long hostility to descend to the earth. So many assumptions of our culture, so many presumptions of privilege and power, are long dead. We are still upright, though, acting as if we are still growing toward the sun, long after the bark is gone and the leaves no longer appear in the spring.

Maybe the time to change is soon coming, a time to turn to the life of the dark, to return to the soil. In doing so, I hope we can remember that whatever falls on our continental patch of land, and whatever falls on the island land to our south, it is all falling on the same soil. Rut Vivian's rock and Kim's seashells, the land of the cemetery supporting Tony's father and the land of the cemetery supporting Kim's father, it is all the same earth, when you dig deep enough.

www.ingramcontent.com/pod-product-compliance
Ingram Content Group UK Ltd.
Pitfield, Milton Keynes, MK11 3LW, UK
UKHW021312180426
11947UKWH00015B/1188